Leagues Apart

Football, Northern Ireland and Me

Raymond Crozier

Leagues Apart: Football, Northern Ireland and Me

Copyright: Walter Raymond Crozier

Published: March 2023

Publisher: KDP

Contents
Part One: Partition, Segregation and Sport

Eddie's question   7

Partition and Sectariasm   12

  The road to partition   12

    Sport and Politics   25

    'A made-up sort of game'   25

My family, football and me   56

  Football in my life   62

My time at Queen's   91

  The Civil Rights Movement   104

  After the Sixties   122

Part Two: Bridging the Sectarian Divide

Forms of Segregation   143

  Increasing Personal Contact   166

Eddie's Question Revisited   177

Appendices   193

Notes   197

Biblography   199

Acknowledgements   207

The author

Professor Raymond Crozier was born and brought up in Belfast, attending schools there before going to Queen's University, where he studied psychology. After postgraduate study at Stirling and Keele universities, he has been employed in higher education, including South Glamorgan Institute of Higher Education, Lancashire Polytechnic, Cardiff University and University of East Anglia. He is a Fellow of the British Psychological Society. His authored books include:

Manufactured Pleasures: Psychological Responses to Design.

Individual Learners: Personality Differences in Education.

Understanding Shyness: Psychological Perspectives.

Blushing and the Social Emotions: The Self Unmasked.

Coping with Shyness and Social Phobia (with Lynn Alden)

Understanding the Blush

Patchin Place: The Powyses and Literary New York

leagues.apart@yahoo.com

PART ONE: Partition, Segregation and Sport

Eddie's question

I was disconcerted when, over a family dinner, my son-
in-law Eddie asked me whether I had ever played
Gaelic football. I was thrown by the question, not only
because I had never played it, but because the reason I
hadn't would inevitably raise the issue of sectarianism
in Northern Ireland. While I was growing up, my
friends and I never thought for one moment of playing
Gaelic football or any of the other Gaelic games –
hurling, camogie (a version of hockey played by
women) – because I was brought up as a Protestant in
Belfast. That is the simple answer. I explained that I
had no personal involvement with these games
although I was conscious in a general way of results in
the local newspapers and was aware that the
tournaments are held on an all-Ireland basis and that
the clubs are organised at province, county and local
club levels. The major finals are played in Croke Park
in Dublin, close to the centre of the city, its enormous
stands visible from the train to Belfast. The principal
stadium in Belfast is Casement Park, in the
Andersonstown suburb.

It is not as if Gaelic football is an obscure game like,
say, croquet, polo or real tennis. It is played at one time
or another by most boys and young men (and
increasingly by girls and women) in the Republic of
Ireland and by a substantial minority in Northern
Ireland, and although it is an entirely amateur sport, a
major tournament final match can attract huge crowds
– Croke Park has a capacity of 82,000 spectators and

cup finals are sold out. The principal stadium in the province of Ulster is St Tiernach's Park, Clones, County Monaghan, which hosted the Ulster finals from 1905 to 2004 and from 2007 onwards; it has capacity for 29,000 spectators. Belfast's Casement Park, the home of County Antrim GAA, is currently derelict (April, 2023) and awaiting redevelopment. The names of these grounds are revealing. Thomas Croke, Catholic Archbishop of Cashel and Emly, was one of the founding patrons of the Gaelic Athletic Association in Thurles, the location of the cathedral in his diocese. St Tiernach was a sixth-century saint and the patron saint of Clones. Sir Roger Casement was convicted of treason for gun running during the Easter Rising by English courts and executed in London's Pentonville Prison in August 1916.Therefore all three grounds have religious and/or Irish nationalist connotations. It is noteworthy that GAA sports are organised on an all-Ireland basis, involving the four ancient provinces of Ireland – Leinster, Munster and Connacht and Ulster. Following partition, the counties in the first three provinces plus three counties of Ulster – Cavan, Monaghan, Donegal – constitute what is now the Republic of Ireland. The remaining six counties of Ulster form Northern Ireland.

The short answer to Eddie's question is not very satisfactory and it set me thinking about how to respond to it more fully, particularly for anyone who is not necessarily familiar with Ireland, its history and politics. This essay represents my attempt to do this. What follows is a personal account, describing my own football experiences in the context of political and social changes in the post-Second World War Northern Ireland in which I grew up. It has been an extended period of extreme turbulence, with over 3,600 violent and avoidable deaths since the 1960s along with very large numbers of life-threatening injuries resulting from acts of violence: shooting, making victims disappear, torture, kidnapping, hostage taking, bombing and arson. Violent crimes were also routine: gun running, smuggling, the drug trade, armed robberies, protection rackets, destruction of property, burning of buses and cars, and car theft. This period has been called 'The Troubles' but the name does little justice to its horror. Local football continued throughout this period but it could not escape the fall-out, as I discuss throughout this essay.

To understand the relationships between religious affiliation and sport in Northern Ireland that made me unlikely to even contemplate playing Gaelic sports you would have to take into account the history and politics of Ireland and the religious configuration of the population of Northern Ireland. These present a complex, confusing and still disputed picture, particularly the period between the 1880s, when self-government for Ireland was debated in the Westminster parliament, through the First World War until the early 1920s when the island of Ireland was partitioned, and only six of its 32 counties remained an integral part of the United Kingdom. Events happened in rapid succession during this period. There were general elections in 1885, 1886, 1892, 1895, two in 1910, and another in 1918; the Irish question proved a significant and controversial issue in all of them. Unfortunately, the proposed solution to the Irish question so painfully arrived at has not proved stable, and bitter disputes continue to the present day. Belfast was a divided city long before the Troubles and this ought to be taken into account when understanding who plays and doesn't play Gaelic football and why.

Nomenclature is one source of dispute and can be confusing for an outsider. Let's start with the division of the island. What ensued? The set of six counties – itself a derogatory term as far as unionists are concerned – is variously labelled Northern Ireland, the North and Ulster. It is called a state or a province or a country but it is none of these. It is a devolved part of a country called the United Kingdom of Great Britain and Northern Ireland, but what significance should be assigned to the conjunction in this title? Is it linking two distinct entities? The answer relates to where you stand politically. It has become a prominent question after the UK withdrew from the European Union, of which more later.

Should the North's second city and its county be called Londonderry or Derry? This is disputed: for many Protestants, the London part is essential, for many Catholics, it must be omitted. (For this essay, I am going with the shorter form, not to make any political point but because it is quicker to type. Also, whenever my father's work took him to the city, he would say he was 'off to Derry', as many Protestants would still say.) South of the border there is now an independent sovereign state but it has had various names over the years: the Irish Free State, Éire, the Republic of Ireland, Ireland.

Turning to association football, there are two governing bodies on the island, the Irish Football Association in the North and the Football Association of Ireland in the South. The local leagues are called, respectively, the Irish League and the League of Ireland. Since the 2013/2014 season, the former is now called the Northern Ireland Football League (NIFL). To complicate matters further, for many years the North's international side was called either Ireland or Northern Ireland depending on which tournament it was participating in, and for several years after partition individual players could and did represent both countries (not that they are both countries). I explain how this came about in a later section.

I begin with a brief account of major turning points in the history of partition and sectarianism in Northern Ireland before turning to the different forms of football. I write about my own experience of football while I was growing up and consider the question of sectarianism in sport within Northern Ireland. I discuss the political events that took place in Northern Ireland that led to the Troubles and examine the role in this played by students at Queen's University, Belfast, where I was an undergraduate from 1964 to 1968. Finally, I consider how barriers between the communities might be overcome, and ask what psychological research might contribute to this process. This is a personal account. I am not an historian, a sociologist or a political analyst. My discipline is psychology and while I draw upon this in the section on breaking down barriers, I acknowledge that I am not a specialist in this particular field and I do not pretend to cover the extensive research literature on it.

Partition and sectarianism

The road to partition

Religious differences between Roman Catholics and Protestants have played a major role in Irish history from at least the seventeenth century. (I refer to the former throughout this essay as Catholics; I should also point out that Protestants are not a single group adopting an agreed position on the events discussed in this essay; there are many denominations including Baptists, Church of Ireland, Methodists, Presbyterians and Free Presbyterians, along with a host of smaller groups and congregations, often formed through schisms and breakaways from other denominations.)

Regional variation across Ireland in the geographical distribution of Protestants and Catholics was heavily influenced by the 'plantation of Ulster' when large numbers of incomers from Scotland and England – predominantly Presbyterian and Anglican, respectively – moved in and seized by force land hitherto owned by the native Irish Catholics, particularly the most fertile land. English military garrisons also arrived to support this land grab. Thus, the historian Diarmaid Ferriter points out in his recent book on the border that 'ideological partition was long a reality in Ireland before the physical border was imposed'.

A useful starting point for this essay might be the Act of Union of 1800, which was passed by the parliaments in London and Dublin in the aftermath of the 1798 rebellion in Ireland and the associated fear of French invasion. The Act resulted in Great Britain and Ireland becoming a single jurisdiction, with one parliament in Westminster. Ireland was allocated 100 seats in the House of Commons and 28 Irish peers were eligible to sit in the House of Lords. Daniel O'Connell, Isaac Butt, Charles Stuart Parnell and John Redmond became leaders of successive Irish parties in the Commons, O'Connell only after the Catholic Emancipation Act was passed in 1829 and Catholics were eligible to enter parliament. Therefore, the government in London was in charge when the failures of the potato crop in Ireland during the 1840s led to what came to be called the Great Famine and the consequent dramatic decline in the population of Ireland due to death and emigration. The London parliament was also the site of the Home Rule legislation, which came after a century of growing opposition in Ireland to the Act of Union.

The Home Rule conflict

When Ireland sought Home Rule towards the end of the nineteenth-century there was fierce resistance to this in the province of Ulster, particularly in its north-eastern counties where plantation had been most complete. By this time, the area around Belfast and the Lagan valley was becoming industrialised and was distinct in many ways from the largely agrarian life of the remainder of the island. Linen had been introduced to the Lagan Valley by the French Huguenots but its large-scale production was centred on the mills and linen exchange houses in Belfast – the White and Brown Linen Halls. Edward Harland and Gustav Wolff brought experience and expertise gained from managing English shipyards to Belfast and within a few years the city rivalled Glasgow, Tyneside and Merseyside in the industry. The population of Belfast grew dramatically, drawing in workers from the countryside.

Agriculture played a significant part in the North's economy as it did in the South. Prosperity depended on a number of factors: ownership as opposed to tenancy, large farms, quality land, plentiful labour, money for credit, investment and mechanisation, and access to markets. All these favoured Protestants, and advantages and disadvantages were cumulative over time. Some estates became large and prosperous. Thus, for example, the family of Lord Brookeborough, who was prime minister of Northern Ireland for 20 years from 1943 to 1963, farmed at one time 29,000 acres in County Fermanagh; the Leslie family farmed 80,000 acres in County Monaghan[1]. An alternative explanation of the advantage favoured by many local Protestants was that Catholic farmers' land started off as productive as that of their Protestant neighbours but their current poor state was due to their farmers' negligence and incompetence.

The Irish Parliamentary Party held the balance of power in the House of Commons after each of the series of general elections from 1885 to 1910, with the exception of the 1886 election when those Liberals in favour of maintaining the union formed an alliance with the Conservatives and brought the Marquess of Salisbury into Downing Street with a substantial majority of seats. (Details of the results of the elections are provided in Appendix 1.) The election itself had been called because of the failure of Gladstone's government to get the Government of

Ireland Bill through the House of Commons. The price that the Irish Parliamentary Party demanded for keeping Gladstone in office was the successful introduction of Home Rule legislation. As the legislation became increasingly likely to be passed by parliament, the anxieties of the unionist population began to grow.

Sir Edward Carson, a Dublin-born lawyer, and Sir James Craig, a wealthy Belfast stockbroker, led the opposition to Home Rule, meeting frequently at Craig's mansion Craigavon in suburban Belfast to plan their campaign. The Ulster Unionist Party was formed in 1905, taking over from the Irish Unionist Alliance, with Carson as its leader. The British League for the Support of Ulster and the Union was formed in 1913. Carson also mobilised public support and a large proportion of the population (estimates of numbers range from 250,000 to 500,000; they included my paternal grandparents) signed the Solemn League and Covenant in September 1912. They pledged 'by all means necessary to defeat the present conspiracy to set up a Home Rule Parliament in Ireland'. Much of the popular opposition to Irish Home Rule was framed in religious terms: 'Home Rule is Rome rule', is one slogan, the significance of which can be traced back to the siege of Londonderry in 1688 and the Battle of the Boyne in1690, where King William of Orange defeated the Catholic King James II.

Extra-parliamentary activities were also brought into play. The Ulster Volunteer Force (UVF), which had been formed in 1913, began drilling. Carson subscribed £10,000 to the UVF in 1913 [2]. Major Fred

Crawford, the UVF Director of Ordnance, organised gun running, purchasing weapons from Germany: 20,000 rifles and two million rounds of ammunition were secretly landed at Larne, Donaghadee, and Bangor. Unionist opposition was formidable, well organised, financed and armed, and it was prepared to defy the democratic process and the law. It had support from within the Conservative and Liberal parties. Seventy Conservative MPs, among them future prime minister Bonar Law, attended a unionist demonstration in Balmoral in the outskirts of South Belfast in 1912. It also had support from officers in the army. Officers in the main base in Ireland, the Curragh, in County Kildare, declared in March 1914 that they would not participate in military action against the unionists if they were ordered to do so. Behind the scenes, they were secretly supported by senior military in London, including General Sir Henry Wilson (later assassinated outside his home in London by the IRA).

With gun running also undertaken by nationalists, albeit less effectively, the position was tense, with the likelihood of civil war if the legislation was passed and implemented. The Home Rule Bill was passed in May 1914, envisaging an independent Ireland within the British Empire, accompanied by an Amending Bill, allowing counties to opt out for a period of six years. Carson had been contemplating an opt-out for six of the counties of Ulster, but he rejected outright the fixed term proposed in the Amending Bill, saying that it was 'a death sentence with a stay of execution' (Ferriter, p. 5), King George V duly gave Royal Assent and the Bill became law.

Nevertheless, the King was so disturbed about the state of the nation, even mentioning the possibility of Civil War, that he convened a conference in Buckingham Palace from 21st to 24th July. Asquith and Lloyd George represented the Liberal government. Redmond and his deputy, Dillon, represented the IPP. Carson, Craig, Andrew Bonar Law from the Conservative Party and Henry Petty-Fitzmaurice, leader of the Conservatives and Liberal Unionists in the House of Lords, represented the unionist position. The conference failed to reach an agreement. On the other hand, it was the first time that partition had been discussed openly during negotiations. However, within weeks, the country was at war with Germany and the Irish crisis could be postponed for its duration.

The progress of legislation had come to an abrupt halt with the outbreak of the war, nevertheless a peaceful route to resolution of the Irish conflict after the war seemed less likely after the Easter Rising in Dublin in 1916, when a group of Irish Republicans attacked the British Army in the city and occupied the General Post Office. Although the rebellion proved short-lived and unsuccessful, the arrest and execution of its leadership effectively created martyrs for the cause of an independent Ireland even among those segments of the Irish population that initially opposed the rebellion. The emerging political movement Sinn Féin benefited from this change of public mood under the leadership of Éamon De Valera, one of the leaders of the rebellion, who avoided execution because of his American connections.

By 1916, Carson and other Unionist leaders had begun to consider seriously the possibility of partition, with the counties of Ulster excluded if Home Rule were granted for the rest of Ireland. In the same year, a Nationalist conference in Belfast voted to accept the idea of a 'temporary' exclusion of the six counties if this was the only way to obtain Home Rule, despite substantial opposition to this within the Nationalist party. The Unionists remained intransigent after the war ended; the heroics of the Ulster Volunteers, who had volunteered *en masse* to join the British Army, large numbers of whom perished at the battle of the Somme in July 1916, strengthened Protestant opposition to Home Rule.

The question of Irish independence returned once more to parliament after the end of the War, with the general election in 1918 producing a large majority for Lloyd George's Liberal-Conservative coalition (see Appendix 1 for results). The Government of Ireland Act, 1920, was passed, setting up devolved parliaments North and South, a general election for each being held on June 7, 1921. The Unionists won most seats in the North and voted to opt out of the conditions of the Act on 7th December, which triggered a boundary commission to establish the location of the border between the two jurisdictions. The six counties turned into Northern Ireland, which would return thirteen members of parliament to Westminster and have its own parliament in Belfast, eventually in Stormont, in the eastern outskirts of the city. Nevertheless, the constitutional resolution did not bring peace to Ireland. In sectarian violence between 1920 and 1922 in the North, 428 people were killed, two-thirds of them Catholic.

Sinn Féin won 124 out of 128 seats in the election in Dublin, but the Southern House of Commons only met once, Sinn Féin MPs attending the Dáil Éireann instead, where a Declaration of Independence was announced.

Meanwhile, the IRA, the military wing of Sinn Féin, had been fighting a guerrilla war against the British security forces since 1919, a conflict that has become known as the Irish War of Independence. The large number of assassinations of RIC officers during this conflict along with an attempt to kill Field Marshall Viscount French, the Lord Lieutenant of Ireland, led the British government to send in the army and to raise two new armed bodies to support the police, both recruited from soldiers who had served in the Great War. The first, composed of rank-and-file soldiers became known as the Black and Tans because of the colour of their uniforms. The second comprised former officers, and were named the Auxiliary Division of the RIC. This soon reached a strength of 1,150 men and was placed under the command of General Frank Crozier. He had served in the Great War, commanding a battalion of the 107th (Ulster) Brigade of the 36th (Ulster) division at the Battle of the Somme. As his biographer, Charles Messenger, points out, Crozier's was a controversial appointment and there had been opposition to it in Whitehall. Crozier had returned from Canada in 1913 and joined the British League for the Defence of Ulster and the Union. He became active in the UVF which, as we have seen, was arming and smuggling weapons from Germany. He commanded the special services section of the East Belfast regiment of the UVF (note the military terminology used by this paramilitary organisation), helped train the force, and acted as a guard for Carson and Craig when there were fears that they might be arrested. He was something of a maverick. He wrote in his memoir (Crozier, p. 15):

> We of Carson's army have been the victims of an ill-defined objective. Was it to be Dublin Castle, a battle against British soldiers, or nationalist Irishmen, or a bit of both? Who could tell? Who could guess? We were merely hired mercenaries, paid to do as we were bid.

He was not present at the shootings at Croke Park, which I describe in the later section on the GAA, but he believed that elements of the Auxiliaries had been responsible. There followed a number of occasions where the Auxiliaries rampaged out of control, and Crozier resigned when his efforts to impose military discipline on those responsible were overruled by his superiors.

The British government and Irish representatives met on October 11, 1921 in London to negotiate a settlement, and this produced the Anglo-Irish Treaty on 6th December. It provided for the establishment of the Irish Free State as a self-governing dominion within the 'community of nations known as the British Empire', a status 'the same as that of the Dominion of Canada'. However, this was bitterly contested within the Irish delegation and in the Dáil when it was reported back. To many, it did not go far enough. It would be a devolved administration (with powers not much greater than those enjoyed by the present jurisdictions in Wales and Northern Ireland). Westminster reserved key areas of governance and members of the Southern Parliament would have to swear an oath of loyalty to the crown. There was also anger about the reality of partition. The Anglo-Irish Treaty brought about the end of this conflict but instead it triggered a civil war within the South over the terms of the Treaty. Members of Sinn Féin, led by de Valera, rejected the treaty and the Irish Civil War began between pro-treaty and anti-treatment factions. Essentially, the fighters who had fought against the British Army in the War of Independence now turned against one another. Michael Collins, who had led the IRA force and had never been captured by the British, was killed by fellow Irishmen. The war would last until May 1923, but the divisions proved difficult to heal.

The border

After the war, details of the proposed partition of Ireland began to be worked out behind the scenes in Whitehall, without any consultations with Irish representatives but involving Sir James Craig, who replaced Carson as leader of the Unionists and would become the first prime minister of Northern Ireland in 1921. The British government did not expect Sinn Féin to accept partition so considered that there was no point involving them in its planning. The Boundary Commission determined the location of the border. Arthur Griffith, who participated in negotiations with Lloyd George in London had been encouraged to believe that the Commission might establish a jurisdiction that was too small to be viable. He was outmanoeuvred. The new jurisdiction in the North did prove viable, nevertheless the outcome meant that there would be a sizeable Catholic minority within the new jurisdiction in the North;

there were also nearly 300,000 Protestants in the 26 counties of the South, according to the 1911 census.

Unionists dominated the number of MPs returned to the House of Commons of the new parliament in Belfast and they would continue to do so for fifty years. Prime Minister Sir James Craig described Stormont as 'a Protestant parliament and a Protestant people' in April 1934; it is often misquoted as 'a Protestant parliament *for* a Protestant people'. Unionists also controlled the majority of local authorities even though Catholics formed a substantial minority of the population. Their numbers were not reflected in their representation on the local councils. The Unionists achieved this by means of various forms of gerrymandering and it was a protest movement against this, initiated by local activists in Dungannon and taken up by students at Queen's University Belfast, that would shake the Stormont administration to its core. This provided one trigger of the violence at the end of the nineteen-sixties that quickly resulted in the Troubles. I return to this in a later section.

All this presents a complicated picture and raises many counterfactual questions. What would have happened following the failure of the Buckingham Palace conference if the First World War had started later or had never taken place at all? Or if the breakdown in negotiations had resulted in civil war in Ireland, what would have been its outcome and what would have been the consequences of that? What if the Easter Rising had not taken place or the leaders had not been executed? Might the rise of Sinn Féin and the IRA and the move towards republicanism in

Sport and politics

'A made-up sort of game'

Gaelic games are essentially rural sports as is evident in the dominance of the more rural counties. Thus, the most successful county football team has been Kerry, a predominantly agricultural county in south-west Ireland, whose team has won the All-Ireland Senior Football Championship on 38 occasions. The agrarian basis of the sport can be illustrated by taking the province of Ulster as an example. Cavan has won the most Ulster Senior Football Championships (40 times). Cavan, Monaghan and Donegal, the three Ulster counties that are within the Republic of Ireland, have won a total of 72 titles among them compared to the 66 won by the six counties of Northern Ireland, where agricultural Tyrone is the most successful side (16 trophies).

The Ulster finals are normally held in Clones, Co. Monaghan, not in the cities of Belfast or Derry. Turning to club football below the county level, the 2022 Club Championship was won by Kilcoo Owen Roes (Co. Down) who defeated Derrygonnelly (Co. Fermanagh). The latter's women's team won the Ulster Intermediate Club Ladies' Championship, defeating Castlerahan (Co. Cavan). All of these clubs are based in villages with populations ranging from 1,000 to 4,000 inhabitants.

When the British ambassador in Dublin asked the then Irish Minister of Foreign Affairs, Frank Aitken, in

1967 whether 'Gaelic football was really a made-up sort of game, not really native', Aitken replied that it was a very old game, 'played a thousand years ago or more' (Fanning, p. 207). It is more productive, I think, to regard Gaelic football not as one of a kind or an outlier, but as one member of a family of football games that also includes Association Football (soccer), Rugby Union, Rugby League, American football and Australian Rules Football.

These sports represent variations in games that entail scoring points by kicking or carrying a ball across a goal line or between goalposts at either end of a field. The sports vary in rules governing number of players on the pitch in each side (between 11 and 18), the means of scoring points whether by kicking or crossing a line, the points awarded for these different means, the size and shape of playing fields, goals and ball, running with the ball, using the hand and head, throwing, catching and passing to a teammate, scrummaging, and rules governing contact and collisions with opponents. (Other families of sports include those played with sticks or bats: hurling, field hockey, ice hockey, cricket and baseball.) Gaelic sports are distinctive but not unique.

To quote the rules governing the game, according to the GAA website,

> The ball can be carried in the hand for a distance of four steps and can be kicked or "hand-passed", a striking motion with the hand or fist. After every four steps the ball must be either bounced or "solo-ed", an action of dropping the ball onto the foot and kicking it back into the hand. You may not bounce

the ball twice in a row. Opponents may contest for the ball by playing it with the hand or by shoulder charging an opponent side-to-side.

I have never watched a game of Gaelic football live; I accept that being a spectator at an unfamiliar sport is a quite different experience from watching a match on television. I remember attending an American Football match at the University of Maryland and found it more compelling and faster than viewing games on television suggests, and the frequent interruptions during play are less intrusive. I have watched a Gaelic football broadcast live on Northern Ireland television. The league match between the county teams of Fermanagh and Down was compelling and the players were highly skilful as well as physically committed. Like all forms of football, tactics play a large part in the game and these were discussed throughout the match by the commentators. Players are allowed to use hands and feet to pass and to score goals but can only run with the ball if they either bounce it or kick and catch it every four steps. This seemed odd to me at first but because they could do this so well, I quickly became used to it.

The 'garrison games'
There is marked variation in the numbers of countries that participate in sports and who plays what is tied to historical and economic factors. Soccer has spread worldwide; 211 countries are currently members of FIFA, football's world governing body. It attracts enormous audiences on television, which has made the sport rich in many countries. It has led to international investment in the major clubs in Europe, with money flowing in from oil-rich middle-east countries and, into

the English Premier League, the USA as well. The recent World Cup in Qatar illustrates this trend. According to FIFA, the final reached a global television audience of 1.5 billion viewers, while the BBC reported 14.9 million viewers for the BBC and ITV coverage combined in the UK.

International cricket was initially played between England and two of its colonies, Australia and South Africa in 1877 and 1889, respectively. The West Indies was added in 1926 (it played its first official test match in 1928. Its side was predominantly white until the 1960s), New Zealand in 1930 and India in 1932. Its ruling body was the aptly named the Imperial Cricket Conference. In 1926 delegates from India, New Zealand, and India were invited to attend the Conference, resulting in the creation of three new test nations. Pakistan joined in 1952. Membership was restricted in practice to countries in the Commonwealth.

After the name was changed to the International Cricket Conference in 1965, the number of members expanded, and its successor organisation, the International Cricket Council, currently has 12 Full Members and 96 Associate Members. Ireland has been an associate member since 1993 and a full member since 2017, and played its first test match the following year against Pakistan at the Malahide ground in Dublin. It selects on an all-Ireland basis but to confuse matters, Irish cricketers play for England, including Eoin Morgan, who captained England's one-day cricket team and has 16 caps for the test side, and Boyd Rankin, capped once for England's test side.

Cricket has been played in Ireland since at least 1792, when there is a record of a match at Phoenix Park in Dublin between two miliary times captained respectively by Lt. Col. Lennox of the Coldstream Guards (a future Lord Lieutenant of Ireland) and Rt Hon. Major Harte. The game became established in the 1820s. The Phoenix club was founded Dublin in 1830. Cricket dates to 1835 at Trinity College Dublin. In 1875 the university side played against W. G. Grace's All England XI, David Trotter scoring a century for the students. It played first-class matches against the MCC and Cambridge University in 1895 and international touring sides at its College Park ground. The sport did not escape the violence of the early twentieth-century. On June 3, 1921, the Gentlemen of Ireland, a team of former 'public school' (elite fee-paying school) boys that had been active in the sport since 1846, took advantage of the presence of the army during the War of Independence to play against first-class opponents, described as representatives of the Military of Ireland. Despite heightened security at College Park for the fixture, two IRA men fired shots into the ground from Nassau Street, killing a 21-year-old Trinity student spectator, Miss Katherine Wright.

According to Hiles's authoritative history of Ulster Cricket, the game to 1830 when the Belfast Cricket Club was established, followed by Lisburn in 1836 and the Ulster club in 1839. The game soon spread to Waringstown (1851), Comber (which became North Down) in 1857 and the North of Ireland club (NICC) in 1859. The first recorded match in Belfast took place between the Belfast and Ulster clubs in August 1840. Cricket at Queen's University dates to at least 1910, when the club appeared in the NCU final, losing to

NICC. Its only cup victory came in 1940 and in 1959 it won the NCU league title.

Waringstown cricket club was formed in 1851 in the small village of that name, a home of the linen industry close to Lurgan and associated with the Waring family from the 17th century, when the Jacobean manor house was designed and built by William Waring, a Belfast banker. Mrs Margaret Waring née Parr (1887-1968) was the widow of one of his descendants, Holt Waring, whose father formed the cricket club along with the linen manufacturers, the Henning brothers. Holt was killed in action in the Great War in 1918. She became a prominent figure in Irish cricket circles – the first female president of the Northern Cricket Union (NCU) – and in the community, serving as Ulster Unionist MP at Stormont from 1929 to 1933, the first woman to be elected to Stormont.

A village with around 3,600 inhabitants, Waringstown nevertheless has proved one of the most successful clubs in Ireland, appearing in 31 NCU cup finals between 1913 and 1995 and winning 22 of them. They have twice won the Irish Senior Cup (ISC). Since 1926, 26 members have represented Ireland, notably members of the Harrison family. Six brothers appeared foe the club, five brothers appeared in the 1983 ISC Final, four were capped by Ireland including Garfield Harrison who won 118 caps. A relative of my mother, Waring Jones, played for the club and we used to go as a family to watch him when Waringstown reached cup finals at the Ormeau ground; we watched him play in 1953 and 1955.

The GAA ban on 'foreign' sports had an adverse effect on the development of Irish cricket. Also, there is insufficient investment or the numbers of spectators to support a fully professional game below international level or the domestic three-day games that would enable local cricketers to acquire the experience and expertise required for test cricket.

Rugby Union was played in Ireland at Trinity College Dublin in 1854, brought to Ireland by undergraduates who had been pupils studying in English public schools. Without external opponents, the matches were internal. The game started in Belfast in 1868 with what was then called the North of Ireland Cricket Club, and Queen's University Belfast the following year; the two were opponents in the first match at the Ormeau cricket ground in January 1870. The first interprovincial match was played there between Ulster and Leinster selections in 1875. The Ravenhill stadium was opened in 1923, is owned by the Irish Rugby Football Union, and currently has a capacity of 18,196.

The sport spread from the four home countries to Australia, New Zealand and South Africa and eventually to France and Italy and subsequently to a host of other countries. World Rugby has 109 member unions and 21 associated unions, and has its headquarters in Dublin. The relationship between it and Rugby League improved after Union turned professional in 1995 and many League exponents were capped for England at Union. The League is short of international opponents of quality and so has been unable to compete in popularity and the generation of income provided by the Union's World Cup, its annual

Six Nations championship and the British and Irish Lions tours to the Southern Hemisphere.

Rugby League is a spin-off from Rugby Union, following a meeting in the George Hotel in Huddersfield in 1895, when clubs from the north of England withdrew from the Union in order to compensate players from time off work, a practice banned by the Union. The two rugby codes became segregated. Players from Wales who left the Union and 'moved North' to the League were banned for life when they returned to Wales and might be ostracised in their local community. 392 had left during the depression years in industrialised South Wales (Collins, 2018); others left because they were black and could not break into local Union clubs [3] Billy Boston, who starred for Wigan Rugby League club and represented Great Britain, is a conspicuous example.

In comparison, Gaelic sports are mostly limited to Ireland and to its Catholic communities. Nevertheless, in the light of the millions of people who have emigrated from Ireland over the years it is not surprising that Gaelic football is played across the large Irish diaspora. There are 83 GAA clubs in England, including 31 in London. London and New York teams enter tournaments in Ireland, participating in Connacht competitions. English teams also compete within England at county and club levels. GAA sports are spreading across Europe, and Gaelic Games Europe caters for 106 clubs, with 95 located in the EU [4]. Factors involved in this expansion are the increasing numbers of Irish citizens working in the EU and the numbers of Irish students studying in European universities. Successful European clubs are eligible to qualify for participation in competitions in Ireland.

Gaelic football is also played across the United States (100 clubs, 40 of them in New York), Australia (64 clubs) and New Zealand. The International Rules Series has been played since 1984 between a selected Australian Rules side and a Gaelic Football side, with interruption in 2007 for on-field brawling among the players. Each country had won ten series up to 2017.

The GAA

The GAA controls four sports, Gaelic Football, Hurling, Handball and Rounders, while the connected organisations, the Camogie Association and the Ladies Gaelic Football Association are responsible for camogie and women's football. It is useful to begin with the historical role of the GAA. It was formed in 1894 at a meeting in Thurles, County Tipperary, following Michael Cusack's campaign to extend participation in indigenous sports, notably hurling. The Gaelic Athletic Association for the Preservation and Cultivation of National Pastimes was set up. This organisation and these sports, along with the formation of the Gaelic League in 1893 by Eoin McNeill and Douglas Hyde, had as their objectives the promotion of Irish culture and the encouragement of the use of the Irish language.

A sense of the reach of this movement can be gleaned from an episode in James Joyce's short story, *The Dead*, completed in 1907 and included in his collection *Dubliners* published in 1914. Miss Ivors castigates Gabriel Conroy for writing for the English *Daily Express* and for declining her invitation to accompany her to the Arran Islands and for his preference to improve his facility in European languages rather than his own language, Irish, to which he responds that Irish is not his language. A 'West Briton' she calls him: he is not Irish because he refuses to regard Irish as his language or to honour rural Irish culture. Terence Brown points out in his notes accompanying the story that Miss Ivors deliberately refers to the Irish language rather than Gaelic to affirm its equivalent status to English for the English: Irish for the Irish nation.

There was also growing interest during this period in Irish language literature and folk tales. The Abbey Theatre performed new Irish plays by Yeats, Synge and Lady Augusta Gregory among others, all strongly favoured in the newly independent nation and sometimes controversial whenever it was regarded by the audience as not Irish enough. The Gaelic League along with the GAA served to create a national identity that was Gaelic and Catholic. In a lecture in November 1892, Douglas Hyde talked of 'the Necessity for De-anglicizing the Irish People' [5]

The first patrons of the GAA were Archbishop Croke, Michael Davitt, leader of the campaigning Land League, and Charles Stewart Parnell, the leader of the Irish Parliamentary Party in the House of Commons: the church and Irish nationalism were at the heart of the organisation from the outset. Furthermore, as the historian Roy Foster points out, the GAA created a powerful rural social network. The organisation distanced itself from other sports, particularly those associated with England, such as rugby and cricket, the 'garrison sports'. Thus, in 1905 the GAA imposed a ban on its members playing 'foreign' games including association football (soccer), rugby and cricket, and this remained in force until 1971. Even Douglas Hyde, when he was President of Ireland, co-founder of the Gaelic League, and a staunch supporter of the GAA, was expelled for attending a soccer match in 1938 in his official capacity.

De Valera was opposed to this ban, believing that the Gaelic sports were strong enough to withstand competition. He preferred rugby (I saw him once at a rugby international match in the Lansdowne Road stadium). It was as recent as 2001 that the GAA rule which banned members of the security forces. including the RUC, from participating in GAA matches was repealed. Even here there was dissent. All 26 counties in the South voted for repeal but only one of the six counties failed to vote against it.[6]

The GAA has a special significance in the history of the struggle for Irish independence. On Sunday 21st November 1920, a detachment of members of the RIC, the Black and Tans and Auxiliaries entered Croke Park at 3.15 in the afternoon when a large crowd of spectators was in the ground for a match between Dublin and Tipperary. They fired a machine gun into the crowd, killing fourteen civilians and wounding 80 others. This was in retaliation for events earlier in the day when a coordinated series of attacks by members of the IRA, aiming to assassinate British Army intelligence officers, had killed fourteen British soldiers. The massacre at Croke Park became known as 'Bloody Sunday' and became remembered as a key event in the history of Irish independence.

A history of the event occupied a prominent place in the GAA web site in December 2022, presumably marking its centenary. Croke Park has additional historical significance. Its pavilion was the location of the Irish Volunteer convention that followed on from the Sinn Féin convention where De Valera was elected as President of the Volunteers. Michael Collins, who would go on to organise the attacks on the British intelligence officers in November 1920, was also present at this meeting. Thus, as Fanning (p. 61) points out, this election combined the political and military wings of the national movement. De Valera and Collins would eventually be on opposite sides in the Civil War that broke out over the terms of the treaty that would result in partition.

The close identification of the GAA with Catholicism and Irish nationalism had its repercussions during the Troubles. Colm Tóibín points out that Gaelic football in the north was an expression of the players' and spectators' Irish identity and he provides one example where some in the Tyrone team interviewed before an All-Ireland final dedicated their game to the Republican prisoners in Long Kesh.[7] In 1991, the Ulster Defence Association called the GAA a legitimate target because of its alleged sectarianism and support for the Provisional IRA. This declaration has led to attacks and deaths.

Given its location in Andersonstown, it is not surprising that Casement Park was used for republican rallies, including protests against internment in 1971 and 1972, and Provisional IRA members displayed weapons there in August 1972.

Local communities were affronted when the British Army occupied it from July 1972 to October 1973, and when the Army occupied part of Crossmaglen Rangers Gaelic football and camogie ground, St Oliver Plunkett Park in the County Armagh village, using it as a helicopter base from 1972 until 1994. This was more than a local inconvenience for the club and the community but was perceived as an attack on Catholic culture. Protest rallies were held, with every GAA club in Ulster represented, carrying flags and banners. (Mervyn Rees, the British Northern Ireland Secretary, called the Crossmaglen area 'Bandit Country' in 1974. From 1972 to 1992, twenty-two British soldiers were killed in and around the village.) [8]

Although the media concentrated on the riots and sectarianism in Belfast and Derry, sectarianism was also rife in the border areas. Many Protestant farmers had been part-time B-specials (a body of locally recruited, part-time police officers supporting the RUC) and when this organisation was closed down by the Stormont government under pressure from Westminster and replaced by the Ulster Defence Regiment (UDR) many joined it instead and patrolled the areas where they lived and worked. Many UDR soldiers were murdered, and this gave rise to the widespread suspicion that, since everybody knew everybody else, local Catholics were passing information about the soldiers' movements to the IRA. Many local Protestants also believed that the murders were a means by which Catholics sought to buy their farms, by killing them or forcing them to leave the region.

Finally, it is worth noting that the GAA is not alone in having an all-Ireland structure. This is true of many major sports: rugby union, athletics, men's and women's hockey, and cricket. This can have its complications as there can be pressures to represent one jurisdiction rather than the other and concerns about which flags and anthems are appropriate for medal ceremonies, for example, in athletics, boxing and cycling. In rugby, a more neutral anthem has been chosen to play before Irish international matches to avoid the playing of the Irish national anthem, recognising that the squad includes many Northern Ireland members.

The Split

Soccer is a major exception in Irish sport. It was originally set up on an all-Ireland basis although this would change in 1921, not long after partition. The Irish Football Association (IFA) had been established in 1880 for the whole of Ireland, with its headquarters in Belfast. John McAlery, the manager of a local tailor's and outfitter shop, the Irish Tweed Shop of Royal Avenue, took the initiative and convened a meeting of seven clubs, mostly located in and around Belfast – one was in Limavady and another in Castledawson. He became the first secretary of the IFA as well as of Cliftonville, the oldest of the clubs, founded in 1879. Cliftonville and Distillery are the only founder members still represented in what is now called the Northern Ireland Football League (NIFL) Premiership. The first Irish Cup competition was held in 1880, with Moyola Park defeating Cliftonville 1-0 in the final. The Irish League was founded in 1890. The 1914-1915 Linfield Fixture List shows that the Dublin clubs Bohemians and Shelbourne were members alongside Belfast Celtic, Cliftonville, Distillery, Glenavon and Glentoran. International matches were played in both Belfast and Dublin.

It is likely that Belfast rather than Dublin took the initiative, because it was by now a rapidly expanding industrial city and three of its major employers were already in business. James Mackie and Sons was founded in 1858, Harland and Wolff shipyard in 1859, and the Belfast Ropework Company in 1876. The Sirocco works followed in 1881. The linen industry was well established in the city, for example, the major employers Mulholland Linen Mills in York Street and William Ewart and Sons in Bedford Street. Football clubs were soon formed in Dublin, Munster and elsewhere, nevertheless the IFA in Belfast controlled the sport.

The split into separate associations came about in 1921.The immediate trigger was the IFA's refusal to allow a cup semi-final replay between Glenavon and Shelbourne to be played in Dublin as was conventional, which resulted in Shelbourne's withdrawal from the tournament. The Dublin clubs declined to play in the Irish League and the Leinster FA withdrew from the IFA. The Irish War of Independence was in progress at the time, the border had recently been established, and there were inter-community riots in Belfast, so it would have been difficult to sustain cross-border fixtures. There had been a series of disputes, alleging the bias of the IFA against clubs from the South. There were crowd disturbances at a match at Shelbourne.

The Football Association of Ireland (FAI) was founded in September 1921 in Dublin by the League of Ireland and the Leinster FA. The IFA blocked the new association's bid to FIFA to be recognised as Ireland. The FAI re-applied in 1922, without success. In the following year it applied to the British football associations to be recognised as Ireland and become a member of the International Board but this too was rejected. A conference was convened by the four home associations in Liverpool in October 1923 to resolve the status of the two Irish associations. It recognised the two separate bodies. The IFA would still be called Ireland, a recommendation that was confirmed on March 14, 1925.

When it applied to join FIFA in 1923, the FAI was admitted as the Football Association of the Irish Free State from 1924. Its first international took place on May 28, 1924, when the Irish Free State beat Bulgaria by one goal to nil during the Olympic Games in France. Shortly before the country's constitution changed its name in 1937 from the Irish Free State to Ireland (Éire in Irish), and it relinquished Dominion Status and the office of President relaced that of Governor-General, the name registered with FIFA was no longer appropriate. It was changed to the Republic of Ireland.

In 1953, FIFA decreed that if the two Irish teams play in the same competition, they would be called Northern Ireland and the Republic of Ireland, respectively. FIFA gave the IFA permission to call its team Ireland in the British Home Championship and this was its name until the Championship was discontinued at England's insistence in 1984.

Because both associations had claimed jurisdiction over football for the whole island, each international side selected players from both north and south of the border. This policy continued until 1946 (terminated by the FAI) and 1950 (IFA). The last match that the IFA selected players from south of the border was on March 8, 1950, a nil-nil draw with Wales in Wrexham.

The most remarkable representative of both jurisdictions is probably Johnny Carey, born in Dublin in 1919. He captained Manchester United, winning the league and the FA Cup, and Football Writers Association Footballer of the Year in 1949. He captained both Irish international teams: he represented the FAI side on 29 occasions between 1937 and 1953, 19 of them as captain, and won nine caps for the IFA side between 1946 and 1949. He was one of seven southerners from the FAI who were in the IFA side that was runner-up in the British home championship in 1947. Within the space of three days (28 to 30 September 1946), he played for both Irish national teams against England.[9]

In summary: After 1953, teams representing the IFA were assigned one name for one tournament (Ireland) and a different name for all the others (Northern Ireland). The FAI teams played at one time or another under the names of Ireland, Éire and the Republic of Ireland. Nothing is straightforward where association football in Ireland is concerned! Relationships between the two governing bodies are amicable, although matches between the two international sides are tense affairs.

The most successful club in the history of the Irish League, Linfield, formed in 1886 by workers from the Ulster Spinning Company's Linfield Mill, had for many years a practice of not recruiting Catholics as players. The club has long been associated with sectarian chanting, physical attacks on supporters of rival clubs and on many occasions, rioting. It has had close links with senior members of the Unionist Party since at least the 1930s, notably Sir Anthony Babington, a Stormont MP from 1925 for South Belfast and then Cromac ward, and Attorney General until 1937. He was president of Linfield for more than twenty years. Harry Midgley, a minister in the Stormont government, was club chairman from 1937 to 1957.[10]

Before looking at the history of sectarianism within the Irish League, I start with an incident that has attracted most discussion in the history of the League.

Belfast Celtic, a predominantly Catholic club, had an intense rivalry with Linfield until it resigned from the league at the end of the 1948-49 season after its centre-forward and leading goalscorer, twenty-year-old Jimmy Jones, a Protestant player for the club, was assaulted by Linfield fans within the ground at the end of a match between the two clubs on Boxing Day 1948 and his leg was badly broken.

Despite some reports that this ended his career, Jones, who died in 2014, returned from injury to play for Glenavon, and still holds the goalscoring record for the Irish League of 647 goals and the record of 74 goals for a single season, and won three caps for Northern Ireland. (He was also a proficient racing motorcyclist, regularly competing in the Ulster Grand Prix.)

Other clubs that have had predominately Catholic support were Cliftonville, Derry City and, more recently, Donegal Celtic and Institution. Cliftonville, which has been playing at the same ground since1880, was a founder member of the Irish League in 1890, along with Distillery, Glentoran and Linfield. When I was living in Belfast, the club was entirely amateur and competed against semi-professional clubs. It regularly finished bottom of the League; there was no relegation at that time from the twelve-club competition. Since then, it has become semi-professional and has achieved greater success, winning the League in 1998, 2013 and 2014.

In August 2019, I watched Cliftonville play a European cup match in Cardiff, against Barry Town United, a club close to where I live. The Belfast side was skilful and well-organised; it drew 0-0 and won the return leg, 4-0. Women's soccer is becoming extremely popular and professionalised. Cliftonville Ladies were champions of the Women's Premiership in 2022 and six players are in the Northern Ireland women's international squad. I turn later to discuss Derry City and Institute.

Linfield, like Glasgow Rangers, was widely regarded in Northern Ireland as a Protestant club that did not recruit Catholics. In an article in the journal, *Soccer and Society*, Daniel Brown argues that this was and is not the club's policy, claiming that there was no bar on recruiting Catholics, and writes (p. 862) of media articles about 'Linfield's supposed transfer policy'.

This is no doubt true if policy is defined in terms of being official and explicit. But if you think of policy as practice or consistent action, we see that the club recruited no Catholics between the 1950s and the mid-1980s. It recruited no players from the South after Davy Walsh, born in Waterford, who represented Linfield between 1943 and 1946. He was capped nine times for Ireland (the IFA version) while playing for West Bromwich Albion.

The club's recruitment practice does open it to accusations that it was the club's policy in this broader sense of the word, since it lasted for so long and was not implemented by particular individuals or committees; there presumably was some consensus on the matter within the club management. Other predominantly Protestant sides such as Glentoran did recruit Catholics throughout this period.

To compare with other organisations, the BBC has no explicit policy for recruiting Oxbridge graduates yet they are over-represented among its senior staff. Only 1% of the population is a Cambridge or Oxford graduate, yet 63% of BBC directors-generals are Oxbridge graduates.[11] BBC director-general Tim Davie conceded in October 2020 that Oxbridge graduates were disproportionally represented within the organisation; 60 percent of guests on the Question Time programme attended Oxbridge or private school.[12] More generally, many women and members of ethnic minorities see themselves by-passed for appointment and promotion in companies that endorse fair employment policies.

Linfield came increasingly under scrutiny, by the Irish National Caucus, a lobby group to the American Congress led by Northern Ireland-born Father Séan McManus, and by sponsors concerned about potential damage to their public image (Bairner & Walker). Coca Cola threatened to withdraw its patronage and Thorn-EMI decided not renew theirs – Brown suggests that the latter decision was not necessarily related to the issue of sectarianism.

Brown's article refers to Linfield's defence of its stance. One line of argument is that 70 Catholics have represented the club in the past. The article refers to Sylvester Bierne, signed from Cliftonville in 1925, a police officer based in Lisburn; Tommy Breen, born in Drogheda, played for Linfield from 1944 to 1946. Gerry Morgan played for the club from 1921 to 1923 and was capped by Ireland (IFA version) eight times, twice while at Linfield. He was for many years the club's trainer and Northern Ireland trainer, and a popular character in football circles. His Catholic funeral in 1959 was attended by club representatives including management and current and former players. Internationals, among them Danny Blanchflower, paid tributes to him.

It is noteworthy how long ago these Catholics represented the club. The turning points seem to be the split between the North and the South associations in 1921, making movement between clubs less fluid, and the departure of the South from the Commonwealth in1949, when the Taoiseach Costello claimed to be prime minister of 'Ireland'. This raised tensions in the North and contributed to Unionist fears about the status of Northern Ireland.

A second defence was that Linfield stands openly for the union with Great Britain, that it has every right to do so, and this might have proved a deterrent to Catholic players and potential supporters. A third, related argument was that residents of nationalist areas of Belfast were reluctant to sign for the club because of concerns for their own safety and that of their family. Belfast is a relatively small city and people know where one another lives. This may well be a factor, yet other clubs in the city, notably Glentoran, are able to recruit Catholics without experiencing this problem.

In an interview with the *Irish News* in 2017, the then manager Eric Bowyer set out the club's position clearly and explained his rationale for attempting to sign a Catholic from Cliftonville, admitting that the club was recognised as a Protestant team. 'We were cutting off half the population by not signing Catholic players'[13] He signed Chris Cullen from Cliftonville in July 1992, the first Northern-Ireland born Catholic to represent the club for many years. Bowyer was manager during a relatively unsuccessful period for the club and he was dismissed shortly into the 1992-1993 season. His replacement, as caretaker manager, Trevor Anderson, made a number of Catholic signings: Dessie Gorman from Dundalk in December, Martin Bayly from Home Farm, Dublin in January 1993, and Pat Felton in the same season from Bohemians, also a Dublin side. Linfield went on to win the league in 1993 and again the following year.

Felton was the general manager of the club from 2017 to January 2023, having joined it from Waterford in the League of Ireland, where he had also been general manager and for whom he continued to act as a consultant. He left Linfield to become general manager of Bohemians and was replaced by David Graham, a former DUP councillor and former Head of Media Relations at Rangers in Glasgow.[14] In his first press conference he touched on the question of fan behaviour, only to suggest that Linfield was no different from Rangers or Tottenham, that the problems originate in the community and that the club must reach out to make better contact with the community. He is correct in some of these points: misbehaviour and racism are widespread throughout football and in countries that have not had Northern Ireland's troubled history of inter-community sectarianism and violence. Nevertheless, the club needs to ask why it differs from other clubs in the NIFL and why violence within the stadium is so prevalent.

His comments remind me that the miseries of the Troubles were not shared equally across Northern Ireland. The most economically, educationally and socially deprived areas of Belfast and Derry suffered most in terms of deaths, violence and being burnt out of one's home. These communities are still deprived, with high levels of unemployment and crime. The paramilitary organisations remain strong in these areas and perhaps are role models for young people, appearing more autonomous and powerful than others in their community. Given the inter-community tensions, fear and violence and the peace walls that have been erected in attempts to minimise these, it is perhaps not surprising that the football club should provide an outlet for aggression that it is difficult for the club, located where it is, to control.

Another factor contributing to dislike of Linfield has been its wealth relative to the other clubs in the league. According to its web site, accessed on January 17, 2023, in the year 2020 Linfield made a profit after tax of £572, 465, on a turnover of £1.5 million. The *Belfast Telegraph* online of October 14, 2022 reports that the club had reserves of £6.9 million. In 2021, the profit after tax was £312,888, on turnover of 1.78 million. In 2021 it had a turnover of £1.8 million. In both years cash and cash equivalents were just over £2 million. In each year, net rents received were £214,000. The refence to rents reflects that the club has benefited for many years from its ownership of the land on which the Windsor Park stadium was constructed. Up to 2012, the IFA paid the club 15% of gate money, television rights and commercial rights from international matches taking place at the ground. In 2012 a new settlement was reached, whereby the IFA now pay the club an annual fee of £200,000 for the right to stage internationals at the ground. Surprisingly, to my eyes at least, the agreement is to last for 51 years.

I have often wondered how the standards in the NIFL compare with those in the rest of the UK and with the League of Ireland. The two leagues in Ireland would appear to be broadly comparable but it has been chastening for Linfield to be eliminated from the Scottish Challenge Cup in the fourth round (their second game in the competition) in December 2022 by Kelty Hearts from the third tier of the Scottish league and for Cliftonville to be eliminated in the third round by Queen's Park, who at least are in the Championship (Scottish second tier).

Even after Belfast Celtic had withdrawn from the league, Linfield supporters continued to be associated with sectarian chanting and violence. While Cliftonville and Derry City have been frequent targets, other clubs that are largely Protestant but employ Catholic players, for example Glentoran, based in the heart of Protestant east Belfast, are also targeted.

I recall once in the 1960s walking with my friend Moore to watch Glentoran play against Linfield at the Oval when we were overtaken by a large marching crowd of Linfield supporters wearing Protestant insignia, waving Protestant flags and chanting sectarian songs, and defying the traffic to demonstrate their right to march where they want. They were asserting their identity in the face of 'the enemy', even though Glentoran is also a largely Protestant club located in the predominantly Protestant part of the city but which has the temerity to recruit Catholic players.

Many matches over the years have been disfigured by crowd violence involving supporters of the two rival clubs. The following, taken from newspaper accounts, represent only a selection. In 1955, Linfield supporters attacked Derry City fans. There was trouble at a Dundalk versus Linfield match in the Southern Irish town in 1979. One notable event took place on April 23, 2005, known as Morgan Day, after the Glentoran player of that name (a former Linfield player) who scored the decisive, league-winning goal at the very end of the match. This was a trigger for rioting to break out with fighting and the throwing of missiles on the pitch requiring police intervention.[15] Similar events took place at Windsor Park, at the 1983 Irish Cup final between Linfield and Glentoran and during a Cup semi-final in 1998. There was crowd trouble in 1990, involving Donegal Celtic and in 1991/92 involving Cliftonville. In 2017 the club was fined £8950 by EUFA after missiles were thrown during the game and a pitch invasion after it finished at a Champions League game against Glasgow Celtic. EUFA fined Celtic fined for five bookings of their players during the match and faced disciplinary charges after the return leg in Glasgow.

In December 2022, Linfield were faced with closure of the ground following continuing crowd trouble. The IFA announced that the main stand for home supporters, the Kop, must close for two months following disturbances at a match against Glentoran on 14th October and if disturbances persist, a ban on the whole ground might be enforced. The IFA Disciplinary Committee praised the club for its efforts to eradicate trouble and the club accepted the punishment.[16] Further violence occurred during an away match at the Oval against Glentoran on February 4, 2023, when Linfield was losing and some of their followers threw missiles on to the pitch, striking two Glentoran players, and the referee considered abandoning the match. In response, the Irish FA banned Linfield supporters from its next home match on March 18.[17] This has been the latest (as I write) of a series of incidents that goes back for over 60 years.

Sectarianism was also evident in 2005 clashes between loyalists and nationalists in north Belfast following the final day of the Scottish football league season in May, when the match result meant that Rangers pipped Celtic to the title by a single point. Supporters of the two Glasgow clubs have a long history of crowd trouble and violence targeted at individuals. Most recently, there was a mass brawl six hours before the Hampden Park League Cup Final between the clubs, and BBC Scotland reported on February 26, 2023 that the conflict was prearranged.

Distillery, a predominately Protestant club, was forced to vacate its stadium near the Grosvenor Road in west Belfast because it was located near the interface between Protestant and Catholic districts and witnessed rioting and bombing. The club moved to a greenfield site outside Lisburn, some ten miles from the city, and changed its name to Lisburn Distillery.

Predominantly Catholic clubs have endured a difficult time in the Irish League. The 1949 withdrawal was not Belfast Celtic's first departure from IFA competitions. The club had been founded in 1891 and admitted to the league in 1896. They withdrew between 1915 and 1918 and from 1920 to 1924, due to crowd disturbances. At an Irish Cup semi-final match in 1920 between Glentoran and Belfast Celtic, a Celtic player was sent off, a crowd of their supporters invaded the pitch and shots from a revolver were fired at the Glentoran supporters. The Sinn Féin flag was flown and *The Soldier's Song* (now the Republic of Ireland's national anthem) and *A Nation Once Again* were sung. The match was abandoned, Belfast Celtic was declared responsible and withdrew from the league. They withdrew permanently in 1949 after the Jimmy Jones incident, described earlier.

Derry City was founded in 1928 and its home ground was Brandywell in the city's Bogside district, which would become the centre of the Troubles and the site of

'Free Derry' in the 1960s. It too has always had largely Catholic support. Visiting clubs and supporters refused to play there during the Troubles so their matches were rearranged to Coleraine, some twenty miles away. The club withdrew from the League in 1972 at the height of the Troubles, joined the League of Ireland in 1985, with a special dispensation from the IFA and FIFA, and returned to Brandywell for their home matches.

Donegal Celtic, a team based in Andersonstown, played in the Intermediate Irish League. They were drawn against Linfield in the Irish Cup in 1990, and the match resulted in a riot at Windsor Park. The club failed in a bid to join the League of Ireland in 1991.

Another Derry club, Institute, that had been founded in 1905, played in the Irish League B-Division (now called the NIFL Championship) in 1996 and were promoted to the Irish League in 1998. Since then, the club has moved up and down between the Premiership and Championship. Regarding itself as a mixed club, it is based in the Protestant village of Drumahoe and since its ground was damaged by flooding it has been sharing Brandywell with Derry City, located in the Catholic area of Derry.

Mike Cronin has argued that the predominantly Protestant IFA has not done enough to support these clubs when they encountered these struggles to survive or to challenge sectarianism and chants during and surrounding matches. Attendances were falling at international matches. There is considerable Catholic support for football in England and Scotland, with supporters' societies for clubs such as Manchester United and fans regularly going over to watch matches.

This hasn't translated into support for NIFL clubs or for Northern Ireland's international side, with many Catholics claiming that they feel uncomfortable because of the sectarian chanting, abusive language and gestures, and flag waving at Windsor Park. Many players who are eligible to play for Northern Ireland opt instead to represent Ireland. The IFA were finding it difficult to obtain commercial sponsorship because of the reputation of its fans. The IFA are attempting to address this with its *Football for All* campaign, which was set up in 2000 and is taking advice from community relations professionals. Incidents still occur, but at least one can acknowledge that the problem is recognised and action is being taken.

Religious sectarianism in football is not confined to Northern Ireland and has perhaps not resulted in the levels of violence associated with the rivalry between the two Glasgow clubs, Rangers and Celtic. Yet the online abuse of Neil Lennon, who played for Northern Ireland and who has played for and managed Glasgow Celtic, and the death threats that he received and for which he required police protection for himself and his family, are unacceptable. So too were the constant booing of two Glasgow Celtic players, Anton Rogan and John Hartson, by Northern Ireland fans that I witnessed for myself whenever Rogan touched the ball while playing for his country at Windsor Park, and while Hartson was playing for Wales against Northern Ireland in Cardiff.

In 1993, Northern Ireland met Ireland in a world cup qualifying match at Windsor Park. The latter's English manager, Jack Charlton, who had played in the England World Cup winning team, recalled 'I never imagined the emotions and the feelings that were stirred up in the ground. It was nasty. It was unhealthy'. Alan McLoughlin, who scored a goal for Ireland that was met by silence from the home supporters, recalled, 'the safest place was on the pitch. You daren't look around and make eye contact. The venom in their eyes shocked me. I remember thinking, "This isn't natural"'.[18]

Here in South Wales matches between Cardiff City and Swansea City have produced fighting between sets of rival supporters. An online search finds report of violence in 1993, 2008, 2013 (at Newbury racecourse), 2020 and 2022. Fans of the two clubs have clashed at international matches, including a fixture between Wales and England, when a Cardiff City supporter died from a heart attack after being involved in a scuffle with Swansea City fans.[19] I observed fighting between fans of the two clubs in the grandstand during a Wales international at Cardiff City's Ninian Park stadium. Football violence is also a feature of football in Italy and across Europe. Racism is also widespread in football, and is common in the English Premier League, proving difficult to stamp out.

It would be valuable to set up a commission or enquiry into the causes of persistent crowd trouble in the NIFL. Potential causes include 'hooligans'' attraction to matches because of the opportunity they provide to fight and cause bother. They choose Linfield because of its long history of trouble, not because they are necessarily supporters. Alternatively, it is ethnic sectarianism akin to the racism that is pervasive in English league football despite the important contributions that black players make to the England international team and the authorities' attempts to stamp out racism. Or perhaps it is a continuation of the Troubles, an expression of the inter-community hatred that has led to the persistence of peace lines. It would be useful to conduct an enquiry that would collect data on the locations and incidence of crowd trouble and liaise with authorities in England, Scotland and Wales to learn about their strategies to prevent and deal with trouble.

My family, football and me

Family Life

My grandparents on my father's side had five children, four boys and a girl, my Aunt Elsie. My father, the eldest of the sons, was born in 1915. When he was born the family lived in Edinburgh Street, off the Lisburn Road, close to Windsor Park football ground, although they soon moved to 17 Harberton Park, off Balmoral Avenue, which connects the Lisburn Road to the Malone Road, a much more prosperous, suburban district. My mother was born in County Donegal in 1916 (and therefore prior to partition) and had one sister and one brother. Their parents died very young and they were raised on a farm by an uncle and aunt. My parents married in University Road Methodist Church in October 1940.

My father's occupation on the wedding certificate is given as engineer and his address as 17 Harberton Park. No occupation is given for my mother and her address is 80 North Parade, off the Ormeau Road. I did not know until ordering their wedding certificate that my mother had been residing in North Parade before her marriage. What brought her there? The street directories of 1939 and 1943 list the name of its occupier as David Tees, a pharmacist, and I recall that my elder brother David, who was seriously ill as an infant, was named after Mr Tees because of his help. I reflect on this in Appendix 2. According to the 1939 street directory my parents were not living at 24 North Parade but they were its occupants in the 1943 edition.

North Parade is just south of Ormeau Park, a street of elegant Victorian townhouses and one of South Belfast's 'most desirable tree-lined avenues' according to a recent estate agent's website. It runs from Ormeau Road, adjacent to Cooke Presbyterian Church, to 157 Ravenhill Road. David was born in 1943. I was born in the house in 1945, the middle of three sons; Alan was born in 1946.

The house is little changed on the outside today; it has three storeys with large bay windows on the front ground and first floor, and five bedrooms, two of which are in the attic. We did not own it but rented it, and my parents resided there for forty years. We had the space to take in lodgers, either one or two young men at a time; initially these were medical or dental students at Queen's University but later they were young men from the country, only one at a time, who were in placement in the local bank on the Ormeau Road. It had been challenging for my mother to lay fires in the bedrooms for the students who studied in their room in the evenings; the house was cold and had no central heating.

My father was works manager of Murphy's Engineering, a light-engineering factory at 17 Cromac Street and 10 Little May Street in the centre of the city. I remember that it was incredibly noisy inside, what with clanging machinery and men shouting to be heard above the commotion. To call on my father I would go through a small door set within a large door, climb up a metal staircase into what you might call a mezzanine if that isn't too posh a word for what it is. I reached a large, airy room with a big window overlooking the workshop floor and a smaller window looking on to the street. The space was mostly taken up by a large drawing table, where my younger brother Alan worked as a draughtsman for several years. Behind this room was a smaller office with a window also overlooking the street. This is where my father was based when he was not on the shop floor or out supervising sites.

Mr Murphy also owned a radio and television sales shop in the city centre and this is where our family watched the coronation of Queen Elizabeth II. My father was a technological wizard and he had just completed constructing a small television set, minus the casing, on which our lodger at the time watched the coronation in our living room.

These were the years after the War, still with rationing, shortages and bomb sites across the city. There was no television until 1953 and then only one channel, the BBC. Independent television arrived in October 1959, when Ulster Television (UTV) opened in Belfast at the town end of the Ormeau Road. I returned from a football match one Saturday afternoon to find that my father had installed the channel and we all watched an episode of Robin Hood. We saw advertisements on television for the first time and would see George Best advertising Cookstown sausages in the late 1960s.

However, there were lots of cinemas across the city, including two on the Ormeau Road within a short walk from our house, the Curzon and the Apollo. The former held a Saturday morning club for children, which was riotous as the staff struggled to keep the children quiet and in their seats and to deter them from throwing missiles. On the screen, Roy Rogers, in the company of his horse Trigger, attempted, vainly, not that he would know that, to lead the youthful audience in prayer.

Action movies, particularly cowboy films were what we wanted, and often acted out afterwards. We watched trailers for upcoming shows for adults and we all booed when we saw a trailer for Marilyn Monroe or anyone else appearing in a non-action film.

The BBC had a monopoly on radio as well as on television and the only contemporary pop music we heard was on Radio Luxembourg, which broadcast to the UK from 1933 to 1992. Many of us listened to this in our bedrooms: discs by Elvis Presley, Duan Eddy, Fats Domino, Buddy Holly, Little Richard and many other American performers. And not to forget the advertisements by Horace Bachelor, a sponsor of the programmes, who offered to sell a technique for improving our chances of winning the football pools and who spelt out aloud the name of the town of his postal address. K-E-Y-N-S-H-A-M. Victor Cardew – about my age, our neighbour's son and a player in our entry games – once cycled from Belfast to Groomsport and back, a distance of seventeen miles each way, so that he could watch the FA Cup Final on the black and white television that we had taken with us to a holiday cottage that our wider family rented, a project of my aunt Elsie.

A sophisticated woman and a collector of antiques, my aunt regularly entered the football pools, and sometimes asked my advice about predicting match results. Winning the pools, which could result in a large amount of money, depended on successfully predicting draws. The pools, run by companies notably Littlewood's, Vernon's and Zetters, were popular because other forms of gambling were very tightly controlled at the time.

We kept in touch with several of the lodgers for years after they had moved on and they became family friends. For example, we visited Gordon after he qualified as a doctor when he and his new wife moved into an apartment in the Mall in Armagh. He would come up to Belfast to watch rugby matches at Ravenhill, which is a short walk from North Parade, and call in on us. I accompanied him to matches on more than one occasion. I remember once seeing him when he was a student, sitting in our living room dressed as a female nurse on Rag Day.

No shipyard riveters or welders lived in our street, nevertheless it was quite diverse in terms of its residents' employment. On one side of us lived a farmer and his family; on the other side, the man in the family was a painter and decorator, who no longer worked because of a back injury received at his employment. (A framed team photograph in his hall showed that he had played for Linfield Swifts, the club's reserve side.) The directory lists a bank manager, bank officials, managers, pharmacists, teachers, commercial travellers, a journalist, civil servants, clerks, a draper, a grocer, a spirit merchant, a television technician and a corsetière and a chiropodist who shared number 110. There was a school principal and, for a while, a Methodist manse in the street before it relocated to 53 Park Road. Several of the residents were elderly, some living alone. A Marxist university friend of mine labelled our social position *petit bourgeois*, which I felt was slightly insulting.

Where we were not mixed was in religion. We were aware of only one Catholic family in our part of the street. Brian, who was around my age, played with us in the back entry and I do not recall that his religion made him any different from the rest of us. Nevertheless, we were aware of it, so it must have had some significance at the time. The poet and critic, Tom Paulin, a son of the headmaster of my grammar school, also lived in North Parade for a while and joined in our games. Tom mentions Brian, who was a close neighbour, in one of his poems, *The Wind Dog*, observing that he pronounced '3d' (three old pence) differently from the rest us, something I had never noticed.

It is difficult to recall the timing of events from early childhood: nor can I be certain if it is a memory or it is something I have constructed or have been told about later. My earliest memory is of my younger brother Alan being in the pram outside our house while I was sitting on the pram. Alan is 14 months younger than me so the image is plausible; I would have been perhaps two years old at the time. I also remember my mother once bringing me into our 'best' front room to be introduced to a small group of women dressed in black and feeling shy and rather intimidated by them. I was very small at the time.

I recall going to Lyons newsagent's shop on the Ormeau Road with my mother to buy a satchel before starting school for the first time and Mr Lyons wishing me all the best. I remember that I already knew him and busy, little Miss Brittain, who served in the shop for many years. Later on, in my grammar school days, she set aside for me a copy of the *New Musical Express* that I picked up every Friday lunchtime.

So, I am not at all sure when my obsession with football began. I can distinguish among playing football, whether kick-abouts or organised matches, watching matches in the NIFL or representative matches at Windsor Park, following results in the newspapers, and playing indoor games, usually invented and acted out by myself.

Football in my life

Street football

We had no back garden but a wide entry ran behind the houses the whole length of the street and this is where we played football and cricket and where the girls practised skipping and played hopscotch. Girls didn't join in football or cricket or team games except occasionally for rounders, which was difficult to play in the relatively narrow entry, even though they participated in netball and hockey at school. The entry was wide enough for coal and refuse lorries to use even when there were parked cars, not that many residents owned cars, and the coal lorries had to navigate the lines of sheets drying if they arrived on washing day. The clothes lines extended the width of the entry and the driver's assistant had to get out and, with the line's pole, raise the line to enable the lorry to pass underneath. On days when we were playing outside, we would have to interrupt our games until the lorries had left.

There were several children of our age or thereabouts in North Parade and we would come together to play hide-and-seek, tig, and kick-the-can. The last was a version of hide and seek, where the seeker starts his or her search from a tin can inside a chalk circle and if she spies hidden children, she will take them prisoner provided she calls out their name and gets back to the circle before they do. Captives remain in the circle until the end of the game but they can be released if someone who has been hiding manages to sneak up to kick the can away from the seeker's circle and they all rush off to hide again; boys and girls participated in this together.

Everyone joined in running races, whether sprints along the entry or, for a longer distances, the length of the entry from the Ormeau Road to the Ravenhill Road. Even longer was running the perimeter of Ormeau Park: the entry to Ravenhill Road; the Road as far as Ormeau Embankment; follow it to the Ormeau Bridge and the Ormeau Road back to North Parade. Another game was a version of handball where you hit a ball with your hands on to the sloping roof of the block of garages and you lost a point if the ball touched the ground when it was your turn to hit it or you failed to get it up to the roof. I recall playing this often with Tom Paulin.

Nevertheless, my preference was always for football. We would pick sides and play in the entry or in Cross Parade with coats for goalposts. On one side of the entry were the back walls of the houses in North Parade. On the other side were the railings of the waste ground behind Rosetta Masonic Hall. If the ball went over the railings we retrieved it by climbing through a narrow gap in the railings. Adjacent was the wall behind the garden of 17 Park Road. (See photograph on page 90.) It was more problematic if the ball went over this wall. We either had to wait for Mr or Mrs Ireland .to throw it back or else walk all the way round to their front door to ask them for it. Beyond that are the car garages mentioned above.

Cross Parade bisects North Parade between numbers 54 and 56, and runs from Park Road past South Parade as far as the gates of Ulidia Primary School. We called this 'the half' and it was a regular location for our games, being wider than the entry yet with little traffic, although there was a risk of the ball being kicked over hedges into the gardens of people we didn't know.

It was during one of the games in the back entry that I slipped while trying to prevent the ball from rolling under a neighbour's parked car and I lacerated my leg on the exhaust pipe. I felt no pain whatsoever and it was only the horrified expressions on the other children's faces that made me realise that it was serious. I was rushed in a car to Haypark Hospital (no longer in existence but close to our house, off the opposite side of the Ormeau Road) and I was operated on promptly under general anaesthetic. This proved a unique experience because no time seemed to have elapsed between lying there waiting for the operation to start and coming round afterwards. In hindsight, I realise that the incident could have been very much worse if there had been a delay removing the rust from the deep cut.

A few days later, my mother and I returned to the hospital for a check-up and the removal of stitches. We planned to take the bus for the short journey but didn't reach the stop in time to signal to the driver. The conductor noticed me limping, signalled to the driver to stop the bus and helped me aboard. He asked me what had happened to me and he arranged for the bus to let me off as close to the hospital as possible even though it wasn't an official stop. Such spontaneous acts of kindness were common in rough and ready Belfast, which makes it the more surprising and distressing that the city harbours such hatred.

We also played matches against boys from the cluster of little streets on the other side of the Ormeau Road behind the Ormo Bakery, the games taking place in the playground of the school whenever the school was shut. We did this until the church built a church hall on the site of the playground and the matches ceased for lack of a venue. (We were forbidden from playing ball games in Ormeau Park, which was a matter of yards away; we would invariably be chased by the park ranger whenever we tried.)

Our opponents included two very good players. Harold was an excellent dribbler, with close ball control that made it difficult to dispossess him. Eric Bowyer was smaller, quick and lively, and he was the one who made a career in the Irish League, primarily for Linfield (for thirteen seasons) but for Glenavon too, represented the Irish League, was Ulster Footballer of the Year for the 1974-75 season, and managed Linfield from 1990 to 1992.

Derek Dougan, one of Northern Ireland's greatest ever players, recalled that at the age of fourteen or fifteen he travelled with a team representing the Boys' Clubs of Belfast to Dublin to play an equivalent team there. It was his first trip to the 'Free State'. He wrote in his autobiography, '*The Sash He Never Wore*, 'In a vague way I now knew that there was a 'Free State' and a border.

> Not that we ever talked about these things much, if at all. Really, I cannot recall the subject of the division of Ireland ever being seriously mentioned down Avon Street. One

thing I knew for sure: I never looked on the other part of Ireland as another country. I did know, however, that the people there – the vast majority anyway – were Catholics.' [20]

(The sash is worn by Orangemen, notably on the march on 12th July each year in commemoration of the victory of William of Orange at the Battle of the Boyne in 1690.)

When I was about ten, I watched Dougan play for Distillery (he joined in 1953) which was based at that time at Grosvenor Park in west Belfast. This was before he moved to England. He made his debut for the club in 1955, while also working part-time as an apprentice electrician in the Harland and Wolff shipyard. In 1957, he was transferred to Portsmouth, then in the old First Division, becoming a full-time professional for the first time before being transferred to Blackburn Rovers in 1959. I subsequently watched him play for Northern Ireland at Windsor Park – he won 43 international caps and scored eight goals, playing alongside such greats as Danny Blanchflower and George Best. After I had moved to England as a postgraduate student, I once watched him play for Wolverhampton Wanderers at Molineux, where he was a cult figure with the fans.

Dougan came from Avon Street, which is off Dee Street in the east of the city close to the shipyards, where many of the shipyard workers lived, his father a dock worker. Avon Street comprises small terraced houses and he played football in the street from an early age. His grandfather had played for the leading Irish League club, Linfield. As a boy, Dougan represented the Cregagh Boys club, based at the housing estate not far from where I lived, and where George Best was brought up and played for the club.

Danny Blanchflower, captain of Tottenham Hotspur and Northern Ireland, manager of Northern Ireland and Chelsea, describes a similar experience of boyhood football. He too grew up in the east of the city, off the Bloomfield Road.[21] He writes that he can't quite recall when he started playing football but it was before he was old enough to go to school, when 'I vaguely recall being involved in little street scrimmages... a small bunch of kids buzzing around after an elusive ball'. After he started primary school, he and his classmates would surreptitiously select teams during lessons to play during the break time, and games continued after the end of the school day. He summarises his progress: 'the endless, exhilarating, unrestricted street-games; the happy wanderings of the little Wolf Club team; the never-say-die spirit of the unsuccessful school team; and the strange unfinished journey into the bigger world of Boys' Brigade football'. [22]

Terry Conroy, who is close to me in age and whom I watched play for Glentoran (in the same side as Eric Ross, of whom more later) and for Stoke City, grew up in a deprived area of Dublin that had a history of producing players for clubs in the Football League and for the Irish international side. In his autobiography, Conroy described honing his skills from an early age during games of street football, often with ten or even twenty boys on each side. His aim was to keep possession in a very crowded space, often opposed by larger boys, and one way was to kick the ball against the kerbside and collect the rebound while dribbling past opponents.[23] The boys' neighbours often complained about the football and once he was taken by a police officer to the Garda station after he was caught playing.

This reminds me how fortunate we were to have the entry and the 'half'. We would never have been allowed to play on North Parade itself; no houses fronted on to Cross Parade and cars seldom parked there. Second, Conroy was only able to play in the street because so few of the residents owned cars. The increase in ownership must have adversely affected the development of footballers' skills. Nevertheless, being skilful at street football wasn't sufficient to 'scale up' to play with the heavier ball on the wide space provided by the larger pitch and on a grass surface and where you have to acquire the ability to propel the ball for long distances. Harold, the most skilful footballer in our local playground matches, never made it beyond this context.

Conroy joined the Under-13 side of Home Farm in Dublin, founded in 1928 and famous for developing international footballers – twenty internationals in the 1960s alone. The club required that its members did not play for any other side, including playing Gaelic football at school. School, on the other hand, disapproved of boys playing the 'foreign' game. Secretly, Conroy played for the school on Saturdays and Home Farm on Sundays. He played for the club up to the Under-17 age group, after which he was promoted to the senior side that played in the B-division of the League of Ireland, mostly the reserve sides of the League clubs, before he was signed by Glentoran in the Irish League.

Organised football

Our family attended Ormeau Road Methodist Church and connected with the church was the 20th Company of the Boys Brigade (the BB) and its organisation for younger boys, the Life Boys. Some idea of the reach of the BB can be gleaned if we consider that the *Radio Times* listings for the newly formed BBC in 1923 included the programme, the 'Boys Life Brigade and Boys Brigade Bulletin'. Neither organisation held much interest for me, particularly the BB because of its military style uniform, its marching band and its drill parades and summer camp, but my parents were urged by the minister to enrol my brothers and me. Obtaining the First Aid badge was a useful experience but most of all I enjoyed the football. I played for the BB team for several, mostly unsuccessful seasons in terms of results but not in terms of enjoyment.

When the Life Boys team was initially formed during a session in the church hall in McClure Street, we lined up to tell the leader our preferred position on the field. The team potentially ended up with twenty-something centre forwards, two goalkeepers and one right back (me). Thus, I managed to gain a place in the initial eleven and I would keep my place for many years, eventually moving into midfield. I remember once playing on the cinders on Ormeau Park in front of a small crowd of adults. I was close to the touchline, waiting to receive a pass. The ball rolled along the ground towards me but when I lost attention because of my over-eagerness I allowed it to roll under my waiting foot and out of play. A middle-aged man behind me on the touchline called out 'bad luck, son'. I felt better because of his encouragement.

Positions on the pitch didn't mean much in our early years. All the outfield players swarmed around the ball, all desperate to make contact with it and kick it in any direction. I spent much of the time simply enjoying the sensation of running up and down irrespective of where the ball was. At some point, I reckoned, it must come in my direction. Passing the ball to a teammate was unheard of in the early years. The ambition was to run with the ball at your feet but this usually came to nothing because of the proximity of the swarm. The ball was kicked by the toe not with the instep or the side of the foot as our coach John Clark urged us to do.

Despite our young age, we played on a full-size pitch with full-size goals. Size of the boy counted for more than skill, as Blanchflower also discovered when he played BB football. Goalkeepers did not have the strength to kick the ball very far, whether a stationary ball on the ground or out of the hand, which meant that predatory opponents lurked close to the goalkeeper to keep up the pressure that would sooner or later produce a goal. I remember once kicking the ball off the goal line only for the forward to kick it back and this went on for ages until he finally managed to place it where I couldn't reach it. I have no idea where the goalkeeper was at the time. Nobody wanted to head the ball, unsurprising given how heavy the leather 'caser' quickly became when wet.

One middle-aged man always hung around in Ormeau Park, hoping that he would be invited to referee a match. He wore a shabby two-piece suit, his trousers held in place at the ankle by bicycle clips, and an old, battered pair of football boots. He brought his own whistle. He tended to blow this too softly so the boys often didn't hear it and carried on anyway so he would carry on too, putting aside the reason he had blown. I'm not sure why he turned up to do this every Saturday morning; perhaps he was slipped a few shillings or maybe he obtained satisfaction from it. Needless to say, we never thought of asking him.

We played on cinder pitches in the Botanic Gardens as well as in Ormeau Park, sometimes travelling by bus elsewhere, to Falls Park, the Bog Meadows, which were close to Windsor Park and are now a mixture of an industrial estate and a nature reserve, to Clara Park and Victoria Park, both in the east of the city, the former in the Orangefield district and the latter adjacent to the shipyard. The pitches were generally poor with more mud than grass, perhaps due to over-use and lack of maintenance.

While preparing this essay I stumbled across a black-and-white online film of a few minutes of a women's match in 1966 between students from Queen's University and Stranmillis College that looks as if it was played in the Botanic Gardens. I was actually present at the match. The University's 'Miss Fresher' of the year, Carol Nixon, was filmed running and kicking the ball ahead of her when it came to a complete stop, stuck in the deep mud. She had to stop in her tracks to dig it out with her foot before she could continue.

I recall another match when we played one bitterly cold morning at Falls Park, when the pitch was covered with snow and slush and the ball was heavy and difficult to propel. John Clark urged us all to keep running to stay warm. It was exhausting and increasingly difficult to sustain the effort keep warm. He produced flasks of Bovril in the changing hut at the end of the match but I trembled so much with the cold that I couldn't hold the cup steady enough to sip the drink. John was an officer in the BB and he walked with a limp from an injury that blocked his own football career. He was enthusiastic but frequently irritated by the antics of some of the boys and told them so often that they hadn't an ounce of sense that 'Ounce' became his nickname. He was a fine man. I always found him very supportive and I regret that none of us ever thanked him for the time and effort he devoted on our behalf.

On another match at the Bog Meadows, we were heckled, verbally abused and threatened by a hostile fellow-Protestant crowd of young supporters of the home team. Our goalkeeper, Gordon Willis, saved a vital penalty and when the referee, under pressure from the home crowd, insisted it be retaken, Gordon saved it a second time! I didn't think we would escape without being beaten up for having had the presumption to win that match. In one exceptional season our team was based around a half-back line of me (captain), Stanley Mulholland and Jackie Bamford, who would go on to join Glentoran. There was no official league but we remained undefeated for months. A rare achievement. I find it hard to believe that all my teammates are now old men, if they are still alive, and maybe unrecognisable. Life has passed so quickly.

The BB is a Christian organisation, formed in Glasgow in 1883, with companies across Northern Ireland, and while in theory it is open to all Christian denominations, we seemed to play only against teams attached to Protestant churches. Football involving secondary-modern (non-grammar) schools was different in this regard. Derek Dougan recalls in his memoir that his school, Mersey Street, played a cup match against Holy Cross, a school from the Ardoyne, a Catholic district of the city. Then and now, boys representing schools of both religions played in the Irish Schools Association Cup tournament. (Mersey Street won the Senior Cup in 1939.) In a sign of the impact of the Troubles, Ashfield were awarded the cup in 1974 when the opposition, St Colmon's from Strabane, refused to play the final at the Cliftonville club ground in north Belfast.

However, when Dougan joined Cregagh Boys' Club it never played against Catholic teams, as far as he knew. He couldn't be sure of this but 'the reason I am pretty certain is that most Roman Catholic boys who are keen on football are always encouraged to play the "national game" of Ireland... Gaelic football'.[24] He only played *alongside* Catholics when he entered senior football.

After leaving the BB, I played for the company Old Boys' team in a local league until I left Northern Ireland in 1968. During that period I encountered sectarian violence in parks football for the first time. Teams who used the parks were not restricted to BB companies but were also used by local club sides. Opposing teams had to share the primitive changing accommodation and on occasion fights broke out between Catholic and Protestant players in the rooms or outside on the pitch.

Watching football

I had only been dimly aware as a boy of the existence of Catholics as forming a community. We assumed that the way of life that I and our community shared was the norm. We attended a church that was undecorated, without religious pictures or priests in exotic robes and without Latin, where we sang hymns from the Methodist hymnbook and listened to lengthy sermons. Men wore their good suits and the women their best outfits – never trousers – and, invariably, a hat. We would go immediately into church so it was a surprise to see large groups of Catholics milling outside the city chapels in their everyday clothes. The Bible decreed that Sunday was the Lord's Day so no pubs or shops were open, and children's play equipment was chained in the parks. No football games were held on a Sunday and it was not unknown for internationals to refuse to play a match abroad on a Sunday.

When Northern Ireland's football team qualified for the finals of the 1958 World Cup held in Sweden, the Irish Football Association (IFA) was opposed to playing in the tournament.[25] According to Benjamin Roberts, a selector who accompanied the Manchester United and Northern Ireland goalkeeper Harry Gregg to Sweden, travelling by boat and train, returned home immediately by plane, refusing to take any further part because of the Sunday issue. In contrast, Gaelic sports are played on Sundays.

I did watch the 1958 heroes of Sweden in action when the team was drawn against Italy in a World Cup qualifying match at Windsor Park on December 4, 1957, a match that became known as the Battle of Belfast. I was taken by a neighbour, who lifted me over the turnstile and I sat squeezed between him and the man in the next seat in the grandstand. It was quite common in those days for lads to wait outside the turnstiles and ask an adult to lift them over (stewards on duty at the turnstiles often turned a blind eye to this practice).

The match was scheduled to be a qualifier for the 1958 World Cup finals, but the Hungarian referee was stranded in London by fog. The Italian management refused to fulfil the fixture with a local referee so the match became a friendly. The crowd was angered by this last-minute change because many of them had taken time off work specifically to watch a World Cup match. The game itself was ill-tempered and the crowd's mood became volatile. At the final whistle, players came to blows, which provided a signal for the crowd to invade the pitch.

The result was a draw, two all, Wilbur Cush of Glenavon scoring both home-team goals, but when the competitive match was finally played, Northern Ireland won by two goals to one and qualified to go to Sweden.

I recently found online a short, monochrome film made by an Italian company that shows the team sightseeing in Belfast followed by brief excerpts from the Belfast match. How different the football was in those days, as captured by the film technology of the time. The players did not look very athletic, there seemed to be little structure to the game and it appeared amateurish with teams regularly losing possession and little build-up play. There was some coverage of the scenes on the pitch at the end of the game but it was difficult to work out what was happening.

I believe that this might have been due to technological limitations because of the quality of coverage not long after. I purchased DVDs at the Tottenham Hotspur shop of coverage of FA Cup Finals in 1961 and 1962 involving Spurs (captained by Danny Blanchflower) playing Leicester City (with Gordon

Banks) and against Burnley (with Jimmy McIlroy, another 1958 World Cup star for Northern Ireland). In both finals there is skill, speed and athleticism on display. The difference between these matches and more recent Finals is how much dribbling at speed there is, with attackers like Cliff Jones prepared to run with the ball and take on defenders. The play was much more open and defences less able to stifle adventurous play.

If the 1950s was the decade in which I embarked on my own footballing 'career' it also saw the glory days of the team I supported from an early age, Glenavon, a club based in Lurgan, a town of 25,000 inhabitants some 25 miles from Belfast. A relative of my mother living in Lurgan was a director of the club and her sister's husband, my uncle Norman, originally from the same town, was a keen supporter, which is why I think I identified with it and not one of the Belfast clubs. I was fortunate that it had an outstanding team during that decade. It not only won the Irish League, still for the only time in its history, it was the first club outside Belfast to do so. They were champions three times, in 1952, 1957 and 1963. They also won the Irish Cup in 1957 (and hence achieved the league and cup 'double' that year), 1959 and 1961. Bobby Armstrong, Stewart Campbell, Jimmy Jones, Maurice McVeigh and Sammy Wilson were members of all three winning teams and Jones scored three goals in the 5-1 victory over Linfield in the 1961 final.

I watched the team play on two occasions during this period, once against Distillery at Grosvenor Park and once at the home ground in Lurgan, Mourneview Park. It was shortly before April 1958; a youthful Elwood was playing and he was transferred to Leyton Orient in that month. I recall the facilities at Mourneview Park being quite basic and I remember watching from behind a low wall quite close to the pitch.

Three Glenavon players were capped by Northern Ireland – Wilbur Cush, Jimmy Jones, and Sammy Wilson – while representing the club during this period, this at a time when full-time professionals in the top divisions of the Football League were favoured. Jack McClelland (Roy Rea's deputy as goalkeeper) was capped six times after he joined Arsenal. Billy Johnston was capped after he was transferred to Oldham Athletic. Others were capped at B-level, amateur international or represented the Irish League while with the club: Freddie Clark, Paddy Corr, Joe Elwood, Johnston, Sammy Magee, Roy Rea, Syd Weatherup. Elwood was transferred to Leyton Orient and Cush to Leeds. Wilson went to Falkirk and Dundee. Finally, McVeigh and Cush were elected Ulster Footballer of the Year in 1955 and 1957, respectively. (Rea also received this honour after joining Glentoran.) There has never been a better time to support the club.

The decade also saw the Irish League representative eleven's greatest triumph, a 5-2 victory over the Football League on April 25, 1956. It was their first win over these opponents since 1937. Rea, Corr, Cush, Jones and Weatherup (then with Linfield) were all in the side. The English side included many established internationals including Johnny Haynes, Jimmy Armfield and the Manchester United pair, Roger Byrne and Tommy Taylor, who both died in the Munich aircraft disaster in 1958. The outstanding performer on the pitch was Englishman George Eastham, who played for Ards, the club managed by his father.

Unsurprisingly, he was soon transferred to Newcastle United and would go on to have a distinguished career and was in the England World Cup winning squad in 1966. I watched him often when he played for Stoke City during the final years of his playing career. Cush and the Linfield pair Dick Keith and Jimmy Hill (the Linfield winger, not the Fulham player and future television presenter) also joined English clubs.

Eastham mounted a campaign in 1964 to free himself from his contract with Newcastle United in order to join Arsenal. At that time, footballers signed one-year rolling contracts and the club retained their registration from one season to the next. The maximum wage (of £20 a week) had been abolished by Fulham's player, Jimmy Hill, the chair of the Professional Footballers Association, in 1961. Newcastle refused to release Eastham and he went on strike. It came to court, the legal case being that retention was an unreasonable restraint of trade. The Court agreed that it did constitute restraint of trade. Eastham was allowed his transfer. In July 1963, he was back in court challenging the retain-and-transfer system and the court declared that the system was illegal. The rest is history, with the Bosman ruling of 1995 also facilitating freedom of movement across Europe.

Nevertheless, the standard of play in the Irish League was poor relative to that in England and Scotland. This was due in part to the small population and the limited competition among clubs. There was no promotion or relegation between the League and clubs in lower leagues. The Irish League was won by Linfield on 49 of the 108 competitions up to 2009 followed by Glentoran and Belfast Celtic (despite dropping out of the League permanently in 1949). 80% of titles were won by these three clubs. From 1982 to 1987, Linfield won six titles in a row; in the twelve years from 1978 to 1989, it won ten titles to Glentoran's two. The pattern is similar in the Irish Cup and has continued in the League to the present day – Linfield won its 56th title in 2022. Yet, despite its domestic dominance Linfield has failed to make progress in any of the European competitions for which it has qualified to enter.

Another strand of evidence is that players in the Irish League were rarely successful when they moved to England. Those who did become regulars in the old First Division or its successor, the Premier League, tend to have been spotted by scouts and moved across the water in their teens so that they could be coached at a high level; George Best is a prime illustration of this. As he describes it in his autobiography, he played football in his local estate, during school lunchtimes, after school and for his school, before joining Cregagh Boys. At the age of fourteen, he joined training camps for Boyland Youth Club, a feeder club in Belfast for English league teams. Bob Bishop, who ran the club, was a scout for Manchester United, and Best went over to Old Trafford for a trial. He signed for United as an amateur at the age of fifteen. He never played for an Irish League side.

Some made the grade if they moved to England early enough. When we were on holiday just outside Bangor, County Down, my brother Alan and I watched Terry Neill play for Bangor's first team in the Irish League as a youth shortly before he was transferred to Arsenal where he had a stellar career as player, club captain and manager and won 59 caps for Northern Ireland.

One solution might have been to increase competition and generate additional income by forming an all-Ireland league. A more utopian solution would be for a Belfast United club to enter the Scottish league as a full-time professional outfit. The NIFL Premiership could remain semi-professional and act as feeder clubs and provide opportunities for reserves from the United team to keep match fit. This is what happens in rugby union, where the four provinces are effectively professional clubs rather than representative sides, and are underpinned by the all-Ireland league system. A Belfast side would add much needed competition in Scotland, although one wonders how much matches against Celtic and Rangers would stretch policing and stewarding in Belfast and Glasgow.

Indoor football

My passion for football carried on indoors. For many years I collected cards of footballers from comics and packets of sweet cigarettes (yes, they did target children with sweets in boxes shaped to resemble cigarettes in those days) and I arranged cards into teams and played league matches with them on the carpet. I played both teams and kept written records of results and league positions. When I ran out of cards I cut out and taped pictures from newspapers and magazines to cardboard and made teams of these. I also had a card of Tom Finney as player-manager of a team of cards depicting aircraft!

My parents bought me a set of two Subbuteo teams, a ball and goalposts (small plastic models of footballers mounted on rounded bases, which you move by flicking the base with your finger) and my father made for me and marked out the lines on a grey pitch from an old army blanket. For some reason, possibly from watching them play on television, I named my favourite side Hungary. Not the famous side captained by Ferenc Puskás to the final of the 1954 World Cup, who scored 84 goals in 85 internationals, and moved to Real Madrid after the 1958 Hungarian revolution, but a later side.

The leading scorer in my Subbuteo league was Máté Fenyvesi, an outside left. The actual player died in February 2002, aged 88, and I discovered from his obituary in a football magazine that he was Dr Fenyvesi, a veterinary surgeon, that he had played alongside Puskás, and was a member of the 1958, 1962 and 1966 Hungarian World Cup squads. Other members of my Subbuteo eleven were Gyula Grosics, Florian Albert, Lajos Tichy, Sandor Matrai, Karoly Sandor, Jozsef Bozsik and Janos Gorocs. Looking back at these men's actual careers, I realise that I would have been a teenager when they were in my Subbuteo side; prior to checking, I had remembered being younger at the time.

Sport at school
My brothers and I attended Ormeau Park Primary School in Park Road, which runs parallel to North Parade, but by walking down the back entry we could be inside the school in five minutes. The school mostly recruited pupils from the maze of little streets of small terraced houses behind the Ormo bakery on Ormeau Road, more or less on the opposite side of the road from the Cooke Centenary Presbyterian Church, which is located between North Parade and Park Road and adjacent to our school. It was a working-class area and the school did not have high academic standards or expectations. (Middle-class families chose to walk up

the Ormeau Road to Rosetta School located in a leafy suburban avenue.)

Our classes were large and our desks were organised according to performance on weekly tests. Those with highest attainments on these tests sat at the front while those with lowest sat at the rear of the class. Once in a position, it did not change very much during the course of the academic year. Corporal punishment was regular and involved a slap of a cane on the hand. I was caned only once and for something I hadn't done and the feeling of injustice hurt more than my hand did. At the end of our final year in primary school a few of us would sit the Qualifying Examination to determine whether we went on to grammar school or to secondary modern school. Not only did only a handful of us pass the examination, only a few of us were entered for it. Parents were advised by the headteacher whether it was worthwhile for their child to experience the stress of taking the test.

I had been a reader from a very early age although for some reason never of the classic children's writers like CS Lewis, Roald Dahl or Lewis Carroll. I enjoyed adventure stories such as W. E. Johns' s *Biggles*. I recall reading parts of Dickens's *Pickwick Papers* in primary school and when I moved on to grammar school our reading in English lessons began with *A Tale of Two Cities* by Dickens. We were supposed to have read the first chapter by the following week; I had finished the book by then and had to sit through weeks of lessons where the teacher's questions such as 'what are the two cities' drew blank expressions from the pupils. I won a form prize at the end of the year and chose *The Riddle of the Sands* by Erskine Childers. I read and reread *David Copperfield* and *Great*

Expectations and Joyce's *Portrait of an Artist as a Young Man* for pleasure, and I have with novels and biographical and historical writing all my life, reading the French classics when I studied French for A-level and at university,

The school was almost entirely Protestant, reflecting the composition of the neighbourhood streets that provided its pupils. I knew of only one Catholic in the school, a girl in my year group. I was only aware of this because she was withdrawn from our religious instruction classes and also regularly left the classroom to meet a priest who came into the school specifically to talk to her. The difference in her religion did not mean very much to me and I don't remember any one else talking about it. I was far from unusual in this. Kevin Boyle, the civil rights activist, who was born in the predominantly Catholic town of Newry in 1943 and therefore a near contemporary of me, claimed that he had never met a Protestant until he was seventeen (reported by Mike Chinoy).

Our primary school had a football team for the older boys that played at the Ulster Cricket ground in Ballynafeigh, further up the Ormeau Road. I was never selected for the team but one day our best player was absent, for a dental appointment, I think, and I was picked to replace him. He turned up just before the kick-off but the teacher thought it was unfair to leave me out at the last minute. I didn't enjoy the experience much because nobody passed the ball to me – perhaps because they wished the star had regained his place or maybe they had little confidence in me – and I missed a good chance to score late in the game, failing to get my head to the ball in time. Football has its disappointments at every level.

I transferred to Annadale Grammar school in September 1957. It was a new grammar school occupying a cluster of prefabricated, single-storey buildings, that opened in 1950, following the introduction of the Qualifying Examination to Northern Ireland in 1948. Its introduction reflected and stimulated the need for the expansion of places in Belfast brought about by the growing numbers legally entitled to a grammar school education following the 1947 Education Act (Northern Ireland), itself based upon the 1944 Act passed at Westminster. The Act decreed that all children over 11 were entitled to free secondary education, the school leaving age was raised to 15, children transferred to either a grammar school or secondary modern school at 11, depending on the outcome of a qualifying examination, and student grants were introduced for university education.

Selection at the age of 11 has long been criticised, and comprehensive schools were introduced in the 1970s in England in response to this – although not yet in Northern Ireland – it did result in many working-class children having access to an academic school education that would equip them for third-level education. Annadale was testimony to that; many of the pupils coming from inner-city west Belfast; Protestant west Belfast, that is.

Annadale was an all-boys school – a parallel girls' grammar school, Carolan, was nearby – and despite its young age it mimicked the traditional English grammar school. Teachers wore gowns, we had a school badge and motto and a school song in Latin. We had houses, named after Field Marshalls in the British Army during the Second World War: Earl Alexander, Lord Alanbrooke, Sir John Dill and Viscount Montgomery.

(All four had Ulster roots; Alanbrooke was from the Brooke family and related to Lord Brookeborough, prime minister of Northern Ireland at the time I was at Annadale, and Dill was born in Lurgan). There were no physical houses or dedicated housemasters as were found in traditional boys' public schools, but they provided a means for intra-school competitions.

The school played rugby, whereas soccer was played in secondary modern schools. I assume that as a new school Annadale could have decided not to play rugby or to play both codes but presumably it wished to emulate the long-established grammar schools in the city including Belfast Royal Academy, Campbell College, Methodist College and the Royal Belfast Academic Institution (RBAI, or 'Inst.'), and thereby distance itself from the secondary modern schools that were also springing up. Annadale proved very competitive against the major schools, winning the Senior Cup in 1958 (when I was in the first form) and runner-up in 1978. We also performed strongly in the Medallion Shield for under-15 pupils), sharing the trophy three times (1954, 1960, 1967) and runner-up in 1961.

I would think that Annadale students were from lower middle-class or working-class backgrounds with some pupils travelling from the lower Ormeau Road and even from west Belfast. The school was, to the best of my knowledge, entirely Protestant. The 1958 edition of the school magazine, *The Cockatrice*, lists three clergymen on the school staff, who taught religious studies. During my time at the school, two teachers resigned to train as Presbyterian ministers.

Soccer was never included in games classes, even though one of our teachers, James Warren 'Ernie' McCleary (now sadly deceased), played in the Irish League for Glentoran and Cliftonville and, as an amateur, was capped for the full international side as centre half for Northern Ireland against Wales in 1955, marking the legendary John Charles. However, and with no encouragement from the school, a group of senior boys ran an informal team that won a cup in a tournament involving other schools; the school never exhibited the cup in its trophy cabinet. I watched it play against the Northern Ireland Schoolboys side at the Ulster Cricket ground. (The ground had been the venue for an exhibition match between Scottish sides Queen's Park and Caledonian on October 24, 1878, an event that helped launch soccer in Ireland in 1880.)

We played endless casual, spontaneous football games with a tennis ball on the playground during break times at school, typically several games were going on simultaneously, and I particularly admired the skills of an older boy, Eric Ross, who went on to play for Glentoran, Newcastle United and Northampton and was capped against Israel in 1969. He managed to keep control of the small ball on the busy playground while he dribbled past opponents at speed, weaving his way around boys participating in other games and others who were simply bystanders. I watched him play for an outstanding Glentoran side that also included Terry Conroy, who would become a key member of Stoke City, playing for the club for 12 years, scoring one the goals (George Eastham, ex-Ards in the Irish League scored the other) that won the League Cup for the club, the only major trophy it has ever won. Conroy gained 27 caps for the Republic of Ireland.

Another talented footballer at Annadale in my time was Roy Millar, who also excelled at rugby and cricket, representing the school first-team at both sports. He went to play in the Irish League for Portadown and Cliftonville, and later became head coach of the Northern Ireland Under-21 team and Director of Coaching for the IFA. He was awarded an MBE in the 2010 honours list. I played rugby with him during games lessons at school. He was out half and I was a back but don't recall him ever passing to me. Perhaps he knew best!

The school fielded two to three rugby teams at each age level, and we played against the other grammar schools in the city and further afield. These too were Protestant schools since the Catholic grammar schools played GAA sports. Indeed, I would go through my secondary school career without knowingly encountering any students of different religious affiliation. Even inter-school meetings indoors of pupils where I represented our school involved only boys and girls from Protestant grammar schools. That rugby is confined to the grammar schools has implications for the adult game. Since Catholic grammar schools play Gaelic sports, the senior rugby clubs that recruit from schools and university are doing so from only one sector of the population.

The dominance of a small number of grammar schools in Belfast might help to explain the prevalence of 'dynasties' in Ulster representative rugby: the families Dick, Doak, Gilpin, Hewitt, McCall, McKibbin. David Hewitt was an outstanding centre three-quarter for Queen's, Instonians, Ulster, Ireland and the British and Irish Lions. His brother Austin played for Queen's and Instonians in the league as did cousins John and Stanley who both also represented Ulster. They were related to the Gilpins. All attended RBAI grammar school.

In 1962, I travelled with Austin Hewitt to Lansdowne Road to watch his brother David play one of his last internationals, a loss against Scotland; Francis Gilpin was full-back in the side. At the match I saw the eighty-year-old de Valera, the President of Ireland at the time, in the dignitaries' box in the front row of the main grandstand, for me a tenuous connection to the 1916 Easter Rising and the partition of Ireland.

Whereas the support at Ravenhill is largely Protestant, the club has changed following professionalisation. The current squad contains 13 players (one presently on loan to Ealing Trailfinders) who are from the South, including five who arrived as Irish internationals – John Cooney, Ian Madison, Jordi Murphy, Marty Moore and Jack McGrath, the latter two also British and Irish Lions. McGrath was released at the end of the 2021-22 season, following a series of injuries. All of these had represented Leinster and the dominance of that province in recent years has resulted in more internationals than can be selected regularly.

In contrast, rugby school teams in the South are predominately Catholic, private and fee-paying schools. Blackrock College, Belvedere College, Terenure College and Clongowes Wood College regularly supply players to Leinster and Ireland. Wesley College, a Methodist school in Dublin, also has a first-class former pupils' side, Old Wesley. Some rugby internationals at the highest level had played minor league Gaelic football. Robbie Henshaw and Tommy Bowe both represented Ireland and the British and Irish Lions. Henshaw attended Maris College, Athlone, represented Westmeath at Gaelic football, and played rugby for Connacht and Leinster; Bowe attended the fee-paying Royal School, Armagh, played Gaelic football for Monaghan and rugby for Ulster and the Swansea side, the Ospreys.

Informal kick-about football matches continued while I was at Annadale. We played after school when daylight permitted in the entry and in the 'half' and I also walked with schoolfriends as far as Bloomfield Gardens, where David B. from my class in grammar school lived. My problem with all this kicking was the scuffing of my school shoes that ensued and which wetting the toecaps did not mask. I understand my parents' annoyance at this because school-quality black shoes were expensive items. My father invariably took me to Twinem's at 33-35 Cromac Street, a few doors from Murphy's engineering works. It was a large, airy shop with a polished wooden floor and large windows that looked out towards the shabby townhouses around the Square which reminded me of Dublin or what I imagined Paris to look like. George Twinem sold women's shoes and clothes as well as being a gentlemen's outfitter and I would self-consciously parade up and down in front of women and girls to test the fit and comfort of new shoes. I assume that my father returned every time because he received a discount from what was a neighbouring business. Otherwise, our mother normally bought clothes for us.

Football boots were also expensive items. George Best recalls that it was only after joining Cregagh Boys Club that his parents gave him his first pair of leather boots as a Christmas present; he kept them all his life. Boots were very heavy in those days and you really felt

it if you were kicked, especially on the shin if you
weren't wearing pads.

The Entry at 24 North Parade

A change is in the air

The annual marches of Orangemen and bands through the city that take part every 12th of July and the bonfires that precede them the previous evening – the 'eleventh night' – celebrate *our* history, *our* victory over Catholic King James. We are British; it is as simple as that. Gradually my views on all this began to change. In part, this was due to grammar school where we had excellent history teachers at A-level who aimed to put our understanding into a more sophisticated historical perspective. In part, it was due to my family. My parents were unionist but my father never joined the Orange Order and I never heard either of them make a disparaging remark about Catholics. His firm was mostly Protestant but did employ some Catholic workers, whom we would occasionally meet outside work and I remember us going to one of their houses in Larne for an evening supper.

My mother was born in County Donegal in 1916 (and therefore prior to partition). Her brother studied at Trinity College Dublin, met his Dublin-born wife there and trained to become a Methodist minister. He served as minister in Athy, County Kildare, and in Dublin. Therefore, we travelled across the border to visit them in Athy and Dublin and to visit other family members in Donegal and County Tyrone. We would have family holidays in Killarney. We were fortunate in those early days to have access to transport, often in Murphy's Landrover. My father's work frequently took him across the border; I remember once accompanying him as far as Lucan, eight miles west of Dublin, and walking in the beautiful countryside beside the river Liffey while he was conducting his business nearby.

The Northern Ireland in which I was growing up appeared superficially to be relatively tranquil in the 1950s and early 1960s. To be sure, an IRA campaign on the border that lasted from 1956 to 1962 sadly resulted in the deaths of RUC officers and civilians but it fizzled out through lack of popular support without spreading to other areas.

Nevertheless, below the surface, all was not well on several fronts. The shipyard and heavy industries, the linen industry and agriculture, which were the main employers in the private sector, had all prospered during the war and although ships continued to be launched by Harland and Wolff, all these industries declined after the war and unemployment remained significantly higher than in the rest of the UK. Brownlow reports that the numbers employed in shipbuilding reduced by about a half (from 19,560 to 9,530) between 1949 and 1966. Whereas, according to Clarkson, shipbuilding, linen and agriculture accounted for 43% of the workforce in 1971, by 1981 it was only11%.

Economic growth and employment opportunities, such as they were, relied upon state expenditure and would likely favour Protestants. Much of the housing stock that hadn't been damaged by enemy bombs was of poor quality and insufficient in quantity. Rationing remained in place until 1954 (I remember my parents using their ration books; I also remember their Co-op number, which I gave to the shopkeeper in order to qualify for the 'divvy [dividend] every time I did the shopping there). The post-war Labour government at

Westminster had brought in the welfare state including the NHS and the national insurance scheme, and the Ulster Unionist government in Stormont benefited from being associated with these developments, able to point out to the electorate the social and economic advantages of the Union. Lord Brookeborough's government appeared to be firmly in control.

Yet political change was in the air. Catholics increasingly expressed resentment about discrimination against them, their belief that they were not treated as full citizens, and the condescension and sense of superiority expressed by Ulster Unionists about them and the Irish Republic. For example, Mike Chinoy reports that the Stormont Prime Minister, Captain O'Neill declared that 'if you treat Roman Catholics with due consideration and kindness, they will live like Protestants'. O'Neill advertised in the press for home help, requiring applicants to be Protestant. Views could be more extreme. Susan McKay quotes Charles Poots, father of Edwin Poots, currently a DUP minister for agriculture, as saying in 1975 that 'I would cut off all supplies, including water and electricity, to Catholic areas. And I would stop Catholics from getting social security. It is the only way to deal with enemies of the state'. This was at the height of the Troubles but it is noteworthy that the reference is not to the IRA or Sinn Féin as enemies of the state but 'Catholics'.

The 1947 Education Act, introducing free secondary education and extending the school leaving age from fourteen to fifteen, helped to stimulate changes in consciousness and in the standing of the Catholic population by augmenting its educational capital and qualification for posts in the civil service and elsewhere that many believed had hitherto been denied them.

A student at Queen's

I started at Queen's University, Belfast, in September 1964. I became a member of a student body of 4,717, 75 % of whom were male, although the genders were more equal in the Humanities faculty that I joined (52% male). Between 85% and 95% of students came from Northern Ireland. Just under 30% were Catholics (around 40% of the population of Northern Ireland at the time was Catholic). Several boys from Annadale also started with me and some whom I knew only slightly at school became friends at university.

Clarkson reports that the student numbers and proportion of Catholics increased over the following years and Catholics formed a majority by the end of the century; women outnumbered men by 1997.

I was also offered a place to read history at Trinity College, Dublin, but my parents made it clear that they could not afford for me to go there. At Queen's, I could live at home. In those days we had a means-tested maintenance grant in addition to having our university fees paid.

I signed up for French and Medieval French (a prerequisite for Honours French) with Philosophy as the third subject. My uncertainty about what to study (French or History) also led me to substitute Psychology for Philosophy, having looked through another student's Psychology text book in the Students Union and found it more stimulating than the Aristotle book I had purchased. I had no idea at the time how significant this sudden, last-minute change in my third subject would be for the rest of my life. I was able to transfer to the Honours Psychology programme at the end of the academic year and I graduated in Psychology in the summer of 1968.

In many ways, going to university proved life changing for me as it has done for so many. For one thing, I was now taught alongside and by women. For another, intellectual interests were valued and discussed. They had not been favoured in school and were not the sort of topic that was ever raised outside the classroom. Furthermore, there was a culture of time wasting and distracting the teacher within the classroom whenever possible and, looking back, I was surprised how many boys who had passed the qualifying exam made little use of the opportunity their success offered them. Many left school at the earliest opportunity and only a minority went on to higher education: a minority of the minority who were awarded grammar school places. At that time only 10 percent of the age cohort went on to university, so those of us who did so were the exception. The high unemployment rate might well have been a factor, encouraging boys to find work sooner rather than later, and many would have been encouraged by their parents to do so.

I enjoyed the student life, even though I was living at home: Queen's was sometimes called a 'nine to five university' because of the large proportion of students who did live at home. We drank coffee in the refectory on the ground floor of the old Student Union and ate lunch there or in the university Great Hall. The Union building at the corner of University Square and Botanic Avenue had opened in 1897, funded by medical students, and was extended in 1911 and again in 1933. It was male only apart from the dining room downstairs. Women students had their own premises at 20 and 21 University Square, dating back to 1927, from which men were excluded completely.

The Saturday night hops in the old Union, however, were open to all, as was the Drill Hall to which couples who had paired off tended to migrate. The premises weren't large enough for the student body so a new building was opened across the road from the main college building, at the corner of University Road and Elmwood Avenue, in 1966, replacing, despite opposition, the demolished Queen's Elms buildings, which were of considerable architectural merit. I had use of the new Union facilities for my final two years. A new, multi-storey library was also opened in University Square in 1967 and I was able to revise for my final examinations there.

I was also taught alongside Catholics for the first time. I made good friends with several, men and women, beginning with James, who had attended St Malachy's School and was studying French. He came to our house, and we shared accommodation in Eastbourne, where we had summer jobs. He introduced me to his friends, male and female, and the witty Billy quickly became another good friend, and we all regularly met for lunch in the students' union. I read subsequently that Protestants and Catholics sat in different parts of the lecture theatre, but I never encountered that. To be sure, in our first year, we often sat with pupils from school but this declined as we followed different degree paths and made new friends. Aiveen, one of my Catholic friends studying psychology, accompanied a group of us to the 'Twelfth Night' Orange celebrations in July 1968 in Sandy Row, a Protestant heartland, without encountering any difficulties. I doubt whether this would have been sensible the following year, when the Troubles were taking hold. That autumn we both went to Scotland for postgraduate study, to different locations.

I am perhaps too complacent in minimising the degree of separation between Protestant and Catholic students or generalising from the faculty or department in which I studied to the student body as a whole. For example, I admit that I paid no attention at the time to the proportion of Catholics employed by the university in the lecturing staff or administration and support staff, an issue raised by Seamus Heaney in his recollections of his time at Queen's. He was a student from 1957 to 1960 and a lecturer in English from 1966 to 1972. He writes of the 'division' between Catholic and Protestant students, contrasting the Bible Union with the Catholic Students' Society and the Irish Society with the Officers' Training Corps. Nevertheless, he also writes of friendships made across the religious divide.[26] I am also being naïve, imagining that the division in the wider society would not be replicated within the university.

Segregation of students was also evident in the halls of residence for women students, according to Gillian McClelland. Riddel Hall opened its doors to its first residents, fourteen of them medical students, in 1915 as an independent hall of residence for 'female Protestant students and teachers of Queen's University Belfast'. Restriction of places to Protestants was built into the Riddel sisters' bequest. In 1971 there was debate about admitting Catholic students: there were worries about the consequences of Stormont passing anti-discrimination legislation. A counsel was engaged to take the issue of the Riddel Memorandum of

Association through the court, and in February 1972 the court permitted deletion of the word 'Protestant' from the Memorandum but did not allow the deletion of 'female'. Nevertheless, times were changing and there was less demand among students for this type of accommodation. The Hall faced financial problems, particularly in paying rates, and it sought closer links to the University. Queen's purchased the property in 1975 without intending to use it for accommodation, and rented it to the Arts Council of Northern Ireland. It is now the location of the University Management School and a conference centre.

Riddel Hall provided the only residential accommodation for women until the opening of Aquinas Hall, a Dominican convent school that provided accommodation for Catholic students in 1944. It too was an independent organisation, separate from the University. Its name was changed to MacNeice House after it closed down and became the headquarters of the Arts Council of Northern Ireland in 2001. The Arts Council relocated to Lisburn in 2015 as part of a cost-cutting exercise and the premises are now the base for the Chinese Consulate in Northern Ireland. It is perhaps telling that I know so little about the Hall in its accommodation role, but I have found it difficult to find relevant material. I know no one who was in residence there in my student days.

The cultural life at Queen's
This was an era of growing cultural interests in and around the university. The Queen's University Festival was set up in 1962 by Michael Emmerson, a student in the university. Michael Barnes, a lecturer in the university, became active in its administration and development. It grew into one of the major

international arts festivals in Ireland, Belfast Festival at Queen's, and celebrated its 50th anniversary in 2012.

I took the opportunity to attend Festival concerts in the Whitla Hall by the Woody Hermann Jazz Band and, on one particularly memorable evening, by the folk singer, Bert Jansch, on November 21, 1967. During the same autumn Festival programme, I attended readings by the poet Richard Murphy, whose first collection, *Sailing to an Island*, was published in 1963, and the novelist John McGahern, whose 1965 novel, *The Dark*, had been banned in Ireland. I purchased poetry pamphlets written by Phillip Hobsbaum, Janes Simmons and Michael Longley, all published by the Festival Society.

Hobsbaum, a lecturer in English at Queen's from 1962 to 1966, convened the informal 'Belfast Group' of poets that included Heaney, Longley, Edna Longley, Simmons, Stewart Parker, Joan Newman and Bernard MacLaverty. After Hobsbaum left for Glasgow University in 1966, Heaney took over the group and convened meetings in the Club Bar on University Road and the Four in Hand bar on the Lisburn Road. O'Driscoll writes that the group of poets now also included Paul Muldoon, Medbh McGuckian, Frank Ormsby and Ciaran Carson, all of whom Heaney taught at Queen's. Derek Mahon, born in Belfast and a fellow student at Trinity College Dublin with Longley, was also associated with the Group. Heaney, Longley and Mahon, along with Muldoon, are now among the most highly regarded poets in the English language. Heaney and Muldoon were both Oxford University Professors of Poetry, and Heaney won the Nobel Prize for Literature in 1995. The Seamus Heaney Library and the Seamus Heaney Centre for excellence in poetry and research honour the poet's name at Queen's.

Michael Emmerson was also instrumental in the opening in 1968 of the Queen's Film Theatre behind one of the Georgian houses in University Square. Associated with the National Film Theatre in London, and showing art house, independent and world cinema, it remains active today. My friends and I were keen attenders at the theatre from its opening.

If these developments reflected the joint contributions of Protestant and Catholic members of the university, sport provides an insight into the divisions. I think I was aware from the student publication, the *Gown* magazine, that Queen's won the Sigerson Cup in 1965, a tournament for Gaelic football in the universities of Ireland. The cup was introduced in 1911 and Queen's began competing in the 1930s. It did not win the trophy until 1958, which may have been due to the small numbers of Catholics enrolled at Queen's compared with the universities in Dublin, Cork and Galway.

In comparison, Queen's was traditionally very strong in rugby union, the first XV played at senior level, and many undergraduates represented Ulster. Ireland and British and Irish Lions stars including Jack Kyle and Cecil Pedlow played for Queen's. Nineteen students represented the Lions over the years and, during my time, Roger Young was selected for the Lions tour of Australia and New Zealand in 1966 and again in 1968 for the tour to South Africa. He was selected for Ireland and the Lions even though he was the second-choice scrum half for the Queen's XV! I regularly watched the rugby team, whether at the university grounds or at Ravenhill, but I never watched the Gaelic football team or followed its results. In my defence, I didn't follow or watch the Queen's soccer or cricket teams either.

I didn't attempt to join the university football club – I'm not sure why – but continued to play for the Boys' Brigade Old Boys. Our match results even appeared in the *'Ulster'*, or *Ireland's Saturday Night*, as it was formally called, that was published the same evening, which seemed a big deal. But the atmosphere was very different in these leagues from the BB matches, there seemed to be anger everywhere, which made me think that football provides an outlet for the frustrations of lads' working life or unemployment. One of our team broke a leg immediately after returning to play from recovering from a broken leg. This was serious because it affected his employment.

I decided to leave the team and instead joined my school former-pupils rugby club. I turned out for something like the third fifteen in physical but non-competitive, non-league games played in a good spirit. I played alongside John Crowther, who had been a member of the only Annadale side ever to win the Senior Schools Cup, in 1957, and represented Ulster Schools. Now John was an adult in employment, some eight years older than me; I recently found out that, sadly, he has passed away.

Terence O'Neill's modernisation plan

My time at Queen's coincided with growing tensions in political life in Northern Ireland, and my generation of university students played a significant role in this, notably fellow psychology students Bernadette Devlin and Eamonn McCann. The tensions followed on from the outset of Terence O'Neill's premiership in March 1963. Successive Unionist leaders openly regarded Catholics as hostile to the state.[27] but when the finance minister O'Neill replaced the elderly Lord Brookeborough, there was hope that he might be different. He sought to ease relations within Northern Ireland and set out to be a moderniser of the economy and the infrastructure, recognising the importance of state investment for countering economic decline. He made gestures towards the Catholic community, for example visiting a Catholic school in Belfast in April 1964 to watch a hurling match.

More dramatically, he invited the Irish Taoiseach, Seán Lemass, to Belfast in January 1965, the first time that leaders of the two jurisdictions had ever met officially. Although the discussion was intended to be limited to areas of possible cross-border cooperation, Rev. Ian Paisley promptly mounted protests against them meeting at all.

Paisley had formed the Free Presbyterian Church and was preaching sermons attacking the Pope and the Roman Catholic church and also anything that hinted at 'Roman' tendencies within the Presbyterian church. But now he was moving into the political arena and proving a thorn in O'Neill's side. During the 1964 general election campaign he led a protest against the display of an Irish tricolour in a Republican office window on the Falls Road, threatening to remove it by force; showing the flag was illegal under the Flags and Emblems Act of 1954. The police removed it after his threat, and local anger at this this led to riots in Divis Street, the first street riots for many years. Paisley continued to harass the prime minister, launching an 'O'Neill must go' campaign.

O'Neill's problems did not end there. He also faced dissatisfaction within his own party. He hadn't been the unanimous choice as prime minister, with Brian Faulkner favoured by many, but Unionist MPs were denied an opportunity to vote on the leadership, and this continued to rankle. He was also under pressure from the incoming Labour government in Westminster, and Harold Wilson urged him to proceed with reforms. In 1966 a series of attacks on individual Catholics in Belfast that resulted in deaths and a fire-bomb thrown into Saint Mary's Training College on the Falls Road was claimed by a loyalist organisation, the Ulster Volunteer Force (UVF). This created yet another source of pressure on O'Neill.

His modernisation plans proved controversial when his first steps favoured Protestant communities, as his predecessors had done. The first decision was to locate a proposed new city between Lurgan and Portadown. Thiis was widely interpreted as an attempt to shore up the Unionist vote in County Armagh. Many non-unionists found it offensive to name the new city Craigavon after the first Stormont Unionist prime minister. The second decision arose from the Lockwood Report on the future of higher education in Northern Ireland. Published in 1965, it recommended the expansion of the university sector. More specifically, it proposed the foundation of a new university and the merger of local technology, domestic science and art colleges to form an 'Ulster College'. (The latter would eventually lead to the formation of Ulster Polytechnic and later the University of Ulster.)

The controversy arose when the report proposed that the new university should be located in Coleraine. I was at Queen's at the time and we discussed this extensively among ourselves in the Union building. Most of us favoured locating it in Derry (loyalists then and now prefer to call it by its official name, Londonderry), where there was already a university college, formally linked to Trinity College Dublin, or alternatively in Armagh, the ancient ecclesiastical capital of Ireland. The argument that Coleraine had available holiday accommodation in nearby Portrush and Portstewart that could be used for student residences seemed unconvincing and short-termism at best. It was widely believed that the intention was to locate the university in a largely Protestant town rather than the other two cities that were predominantly Catholic. It seemed to many of us students to be yet another example of Unionist gerrymandering.

The Civil Rights movement

O'Neill also encountered problems with an emerging civil rights movement, consciously modelled on the American movement that had recently become active, notably the marches to Selma and to Washington DC. What was distinctive about this within the tradition of Northern Ireland protests, was that it was not about constitutional matters, partition and existence of the jurisdiction, but about discrimination against Catholics on equal voting rights, honest elections and fair allocation of public housing. These were all issues that people across Great Britain and abroad would regard as unproblematic and would find it difficult to believe that the Stormont government would react with such strident opposition.

Nor is there evidence that discrimination in public housing was widespread across Northern Ireland, although there were examples, notably in Dungannon.

There were slightly more Catholics than Protestants in the town but the numbers of houses allocated by the local council between 1945 and 1963 were 34 to Catholics and 264 to Protestants. Notwithstanding these statistics, many loyalists regarded the emerging civil rights movement as subversive and served as a front or a pawn of Republicanism. They argued that the number of Catholics who were to the fore in the protests merely proved their point, as did the number of Communists and Trotskyists alleged to be among its youthful leadership.

The movement began in a small way when Conn and Pamela McCluskey, a GP and his wife from Dungannon, protested against unjust allocation of public housing and set up the Homeless Citizen's League in 1963, organising a march and squatting in a local bungalow. They next set up the Campaign for Social Justice to document and publicise cases of discrimination.

In Westminster, the Campaign for Democracy in Ulster was launched in 1965 by a group of Labour MPs and functioned, along with Gerry Fitt of the Republican Labour Party, who was elected as MP for Belfast West, as a pressure group on Prime Minister Harold Wilson to intervene to right these injustices. Intervention would be in contradiction to the Westminster convention not to interfere with matters that were devolved to Stormont, a convention that enabled the Stormont government to avoid scrutiny of these practices. In another step, the Northern Ireland Civil Rights Association (NICRA) was formed on January 29, 1967, at a meeting of around100 people in the International Hotel in Belfast's city centre, with Dr McCluskey elected as vice-chairman.

The organisation held its first march, from Coalisland to Dungannon, in June 1968, encountering protests by Paisley's supporters. On June 20, 1968, Austin Currie, a Queen's graduate, cofounder of the Social Democratic and Labour Party and Stormont MP from May 1964 until the suspension of Stormont in 1972, squatted in a council house in Coalisland that had been allocated to a single Protestant woman, secretary to a local Unionist MP, despite there being a lengthy waiting list of Catholic families in need of housing. The protest received widespread coverage by the media, drawing further attention to discrimination in the allocation of public housing within Northern Ireland.

What ensued was a series of marches in rapid succession that culminated in what became known as the Battle of Burntollet Bridge in January 1969, the aftermath of which would drive Northern Ireland to the brink of outright civil war and the deployment on the streets of the British Army.

A second march took place on 5th October in Derry. William Craig, the Stormont Minister of Home Affairs, banned the march along with an Apprentice Boys meeting scheduled for the same day. The march went ahead, with three Labour MPs from Westminster, Gerry Fitt, and Queen's University psychology student Bernadette Devlin in its ranks. The RUC blocked their progress and when the marchers attempted to break through, the police officers attacked them with clubs and water cannon. Subsequent riots spread across the city centre into the Catholic Bogside district.

The marchers were not deterred and another march involving 2,000 students took place on 9th October, from Queen's University to Belfast City Hall. Paisley organised a counter-demonstration and the RUC blocked the students, preventing them from following the previously agreed route. The students responded with a sit-in in Linenhall Street behind the City Hall. When the angry and frustrated students returned to the university, they held a large meeting in the McMordie Hall of the Students' Union where the People's Democracy (PD) movement was formed that included undergraduates Michael Farrell, Bernadette Devlin and Eamonn McCann, and a young law lecturer, Kevin Boyle.

Subsequent marches were held on 16th October in Derry, on 4th November to Belfast City Hall and on 30th of the month through the city of Armagh. All followed a similar pattern; a route would be agreed with the RUC; Paisleyites would arrange a counter-demonstration and the police would insist on rerouting the march. This would result in violence involving police officers or Paisleyites or both. Thus, lawful marches were repeatedly prevented by threats or actual violence. In December, O'Neill, already weak and losing control over his party, made a conciliatory speech that encouraged the NICRA and PD to suspend marches and he sacked his hardliner minister, Craig. But things had already gone too far.

The most damaging PD march in many senses set off at the beginning of the new year from Belfast to Derry. It was harassed by loyalists from the outset but the main body of the march was ambushed on 4th January at Burntollet Bridge, about six miles from Derry. A large crowd of loyalists that included off-duty B-special policemen attacked the young men and women with clubs and blocks of wood with nails in them while the RUC officers made little attempt to disperse the loyalists or prevent them from attacking. Several marchers were injured and taken to hospital. News of this led to riots in Derry and from then on rioting became regular in Belfast and Derry, with the RUC entering Catholic areas and, in the process, enabling a Protestant mob to follow them in. The riots reached a peak in August, during the annual Apprentice Boys march that the government and police had allowed to go ahead.

O'Neill had already resigned, on 28th April, after the Unionist Party performed poorly in the election that he called in an attempt to shore up his support. One man-one vote had only been passed by a narrow majority in Stormont on the 22nd April, and James Chichester-Clark, O'Neill's deputy, resigned in protest at the decision. He succeeded O'Neill as prime minister, and one of his first duties was to call in the British Army to quell the rioting. The Army would not leave the province for thirty years, growing from a standing garrison of 2,000 to 7,500 by September 2016 (Henry Patterson, p. 217) and becoming increasingly inserted into the landscape and embedded in the fabric of daily life. Stronger leaders than O'Neill and Chichester-Clark including Faulkner and David Trimble would in time prove no more successful in keeping the Ulster Unionist Party (UUP) together or impeding Paisley's relentless progress to the office of first minister and the Democratic Unionist Party (DUP) dominance of unionism.

The involvement of Queen's students
The years from 1963 to 1969 proved critical leading up to the years of excessive violence in Northern Ireland. People's Democracy, the movement originating in

Queen's, has been blamed for starting the Troubles. They proved a trigger for the violence although hardly the underlying cause. This, or rather multiple causes, I have suggested, can be traced back through centuries to the plantation of Ulster; the long struggle for Irish independence; unionist opposition to parliamentary processes aiming to bring about Home Rule, prepared to use violent means to do so; the Easter Rising; the Irish War of Independence; partition; the intransigence of successive Unionist governments at Stormont.

Sectarian attacks and riots were not new in the 1960s. There were attacks throughout the eighteenth and nineteenth centuries, described by Seamus Mallon in his autobiography. In *A History of the Belfast Riots* published in 1864, Thomas Henry described rioting in Belfast in that year involving residents of Sandy Row and Pound Loaning, where the residents of the Pound 'stole along Durham-Street, armed with bludgeons and pistols'. [28] There was widespread rioting and attacks by Protestants on Catholic areas in the 1920s during the Irish War of Independence. The violence was not confined to Belfast but reached Antrim, Banbridge, Bangor, Dromore, Lisburn and Newtownards.

More than seven thousand Catholic and Protestant workers who were regarded as radicals or communists and as insufficiently sectarian were forcibly expelled from the shipyards in Belfast in July 1920. Victims were thrown into the dock and pelted with sawn-off rivets – so called 'Belfast confetti'. Attacks on Catholic areas were often triggered by murders of police officers by the IRA, for example Glenn Patterson describes the Swanzy riots and looting of Catholic areas in Lisburn in August 1920 that followed the assassination of Inspector Swanzy by members of the Cork and Belfast

IRA. There were riots in Belfast in 1935, where 514 Catholic families were evicted, 431 violently and 73 burned out.[29] There is perhaps a 'collective folk memory' of invasions of Catholic districts.

The emerging independent Ireland was built on violence – the 1916 Rising, the War of Independence and the Irish Civil War – and there is no doubt that the Unionists were prepared to use violence to defy the British government in the early years of the twentieth century if there had been an attempt to impose Home Rule.

Yet there are allegations that the actions of the students served as an immediate cause, a trigger. Were they politically and culturally naïve in their actions? Should they have been more aware how contentious marches would be among the loyalist communities? Were they unwittingly poking the dozing bear, so to speak? Didn't they realise that there were more dangerous opponents to the civil rights cause than Captain O'Neill could be? Wasn't Paisley's ability to mobilise large numbers of his supporters sufficient warning of that? What in any case would be gained by undermining or removing the moderate O'Neill? And what exactly were their aims: What did they hope to achieve by their marches through Belfast, Derry and Armagh?

First, it is worth pointing out that political marches have a history, not only in the United States, where the potential for change produced by the Selma and Washington marches and rallies influenced the NICRA and PD, but also in Britain: the Suffragette Pilgrimages, the Jarrow March, the Aldermaston CND marches, marches during the Coal Miners' strike of

1984-85, marches against the war in Iraq and, from the right of the political spectrum, the Countryside Alliance. Participation in marches does not necessarily have a single goal but can serve many purposes in pursuit of various goals. It is a form of public demonstration is support of a cause; it is action in the public sphere rather than behind the closed doors of meeting rooms; it gains media attention; it sends a signal to government, particularly in this case, the UK government and Westminster MPs; it shows itself and what it stands for to the public; it aims to raise support; it promotes commitment and togetherness among the marchers; it provides an outlet for emotion. A positive reception is rewarding; a hostile response can be motivating.

Resentment is a powerful driver of political behaviour. The PD resented that the Orange Order and Apprentice Boys along with Paisley supporters regard it as their right to walk the streets of Northern Ireland while denying the same right to their opponents. Resentment among the population has brought down governments: the Poll Tax brought down the seemingly impregnable Margaret Thatcher; 'partygate' was instrumental in removing Boris Johnson from office.

The civil rights loose coalition was never a well-organised, disciplined, top-down movement. The circumstances of the origin of PD illustrates this. It involved diverse individuals and positions, republicans, Trotskyists, members of Queen's University Socialist Alliance, and civil rights activists like Kevin Boyle, who would become an internationally respected human rights lawyer. The diversity made long-term policy making virtually impossible in the short time-scale involved. This was undoubtedly a major weakness. For example, the PD called off a planned march when they heard O'Neill's conciliatory speech about Ulster 'at the crossroads' yet they were on the road again a couple of weeks later, setting out on the fateful journey to Burntollet Bridge. This would play into the hands of government spokespersons like William Craig, who alleged that 'NICRA…was a front for republicans and communists with a hidden anti-partitionist agenda' (Henry Patterson, p. 203). Yet the explicit aim of MICRA and PD was reform of Northern Ireland, not reunification.

Republicans, North and South, including the IRA, did have an interest in the campaign, particularly after it received international media attention and stimulated a hitherto reluctant British government to devote time to Northern Ireland affairs. The main spur to republican action was the spread of the post-march riots to the Catholic enclaves of Belfast and Derry, the incursions by the RUC into these enclaves followed by attacks from Protestant mobs and the involvement of the British Army. The first attempts to defend the enclaves were feeble and attracted the scornful remark that IRA stood for 'I Ran Away'. But before long the IRA became organised, entrenched, armed and dangerous, and the rest is history.

The Cameron Report of 1969, set up by O'Neill, reported on the marches and their sequel and concluded that many leaders of NICRA had ambitions beyond their expressed one and treated this aim as a 'stalking horse' for their goals of abolishing the border and unifying Ireland as an 'all-Ireland Workers Socialist Republic (paragraph 189). One paragraph was devoted solely to pointing out that the leadership and most of the members were Roman Catholic (para. 192); Was this something of a 'dog whistle', a message for those with ears to hear? The Report rejected the PD's claim of spontaneous, democratic decision-making and concluded that their polces would lead to the breakup of the current constitutional position of Northern Ireland (para., 120). It argued that this would be aided by PD's decision to open the membership to non-members of the University, with the risk of infiltration. Cameron nevertheless did acknowledge that Farrell and McCann were prepared to urge their supporters to avoid violence; the report is less clear about Devlin's stance on this (para. 195).

Cameron also reported on the Derry Citizen's Action Committee (where McCann was also prominent along with John Hume, whom the report praised for his restraint and who eventually won the Nobel Peace Prize alongside David Trimble for their endeavours in Northern Ireland); the IRA; Paisley and the Ulster Constitution Defence Committee and the Ulster Protestant Volunteers The report concluded that Paisley, Major Bunting and these organisations bore major responsibility for the disorders in Armagh and Burntollet Bridge and for their obstruction of what might have otherwise been peaceful and controllable demonstrations.

Moving on from the membership of these organisations, the Report considered the causes of the disorders. It noted, more broadly, changes within the Catholic community and the rise of an educated middle class; it acknowledged the rising sense of injustice, grievance and resentment among the Catholic population, and the fears of Protestants that Unionist dominance and partition were at risk. More specifically, it drew attention to resentment about the rerouting of the march in Londonderry on 5th October 1968 and to poor policing throughout the events and in particular at Burntollet Bridge. Police Inspector Meharg gave evidence to the Commission and subsequently denied that the police had led the marchers into an ambush but instead had warned them of the dangers they faced. The report roundly condemned the PD. It was, it concluded, the transformation of a students' demonstration on civil rights into the People's Democracy, 'itself an unnecessary adjunct' to NICRA, that provided a means for politically motivated extremists to incite disorder with the counterproductive result that opposition to the civil rights movement and its cause increased. On the other side, Paisley and his colleague Major Bunting were also strongly criticised for their supporters contributing to the violence and hampering the police in their control of demonstrations.

The Report makes much of the Trotskyist, socialist and republican background of the leaders of the civil rights movements. However, it should be taken into account that people who adhere to these political positions have the same right as anyone else to participate in demonstrations that were approved by the authorities. Furthermore, the Protestant *and* the Catholic areas protesting about housing and other forms of discrimination were among the most economically and socially deprived parts of the United Kingdom so it is unsurprising that individuals who volunteer to lead the protests are those motivated to change the system that has contributed to this deprivation. This is particularly the case when grievances are legitimate (as the Report concludes) and when deprived areas are in conflict with one another.

The test of the sincerity of the leaders of the protests is straightforward; address the grievances and see where the leaders stand. Again, the unionist policies of 'Not an Inch' and 'Ulster Says No' obstructed this.

Undoubtedly, mistakes were made on all sides, resulting in rioting on a daily basis, greater sectarianism than before, more separation of housing into single-religious neighbourhoods, murders of individuals, assassinations of groups of people, attacks on the police and armed forces, and bombing campaigns directed at city centre stores, restaurants, pubs, places where innocent people gathered. What is so striking to me is the depth of hatred that lay underneath the apparently tranquil face of Northern Ireland when I was growing up. Certainly, I was aware of, read about and witnessed gang fights between Protestant and Catholic youths; I once saw RUC officers using batons to break up a crowd of Catholic youths just off Shaftesbury Square. I was familiar with the routine name-calling of Catholics as Fenians and Taigs but the hatred seemed to run much deeper than that.

The travel writer, Dervla Murphy, described in her book *A Place Apart: Northern Ireland in the 1970s* listening to a sermon by Paisley in his church on the Ravenhill Road and being horrified and frightened by the views she heard expressed and the nature of the response of the packed congregation. Any threat to unionist hegemony, of Catholics failing to keep their place, was certain to produce an extreme reaction and the tradition of violence that underpinned the Irish War of Independence and Irish Civil War showed that violence would be met with violence and that guerrilla and underground tactics would prevail.

Shortly after I started at Queen's in September 1964, steps towards the Troubles were already being taken, although few would have anticipated the full implications or the ultimate destination of those steps at the time. I read in the *Belfast Telegraph* and watched the television news coverage of the removal of the Irish tricolour and the ensuing Divis Street riots that took place in the same month.

Peter Berresford Ellis, a young journalist visiting Belfast at the time provided an eyewitness report (quoted by Paul Megven):

> On the Sunday, 27 September… Paisley had called a meeting at the Ulster Hall, having heard of the flag in the window of the Sinn Féin campaign headquarters. He declared that if the RUC did not remove the flag, he would lead his followers in an attack on the election office. The Stormont minister of home affairs, R W McConnell, actually went in person to see Paisley to placate him and assure him that the RUC would go in. The day after I arrived 'wide eyed' in Belfast, district inspector Frank Lagan and fifty RUC men – the first time I had seen such heavily armed police in what was supposed to be part of the United Kingdom – smashed in the door of the election office, confiscated the flag and generally destroyed everything they could lay their hands on. A few days later the flag was displayed again in defiance and the RUC were soon back with pick axes. This time the office was destroyed beyond salvage…That night protests turned to rioting in West Belfast. The RUC then astounded the world by going into

action with armoured cars, mounted with guns and water cannons lines advanced like storm troopers.

A national General Election was held in October, resulting in victory for the Labour Party under Harold Wilson. Might things have turned out differently had the Conservatives remained in office, with their traditional sympathies towards unionism? The O'Neill-Lemass meetings took place the following year; Paisley's protest demonstration against the meetings was another sign of loyalist obduracy. In 1966, the Ulster Volunteer Force (UVF) became active and their members were responsible for the death of a 77-year-old Protestant woman from injuries received from a UVF firebomb in May 1966; they murdered two men in June, in the same month that Paisley supporters and Catholics had rioted in Cromac Square. The NICRA was formed in January 1967 and held its first march from Coalisland to Dungannon in August.

1968 was my final year, so I was preoccupied at this time with completing my dissertation and revising for the set of final examinations, which ended on 29th May in time for me to go to the Students Union to watch on television George Best star in Manchester United's victory in the European Cup Final that evening. In my first year I had joined the New Ireland Society and attended debates of the Literary and Scientific (''Literific') Society, largely because of my interest in Irish history rather than any desire to participate in political life. This was, I think, before Eamonn McCann became president of the Literific. I don't know that I would agree with the historian Henry Patterson's assertion that Queen's had been 'one of the most docile campuses in Western Europe' but certainly there were few overt signs of unusual political activity in the Union. This was to change dramatically before the year was out.

After graduation, I had a vacation with university friends in Tarragona before heading in September to Stirling University in Scotland. I heard news of the PD marches from friends who were still at Queen's and of course through the media in England and Scotland, which now devoted considerable attention to Northern Ireland, having neglected it for years. Eventually, the Troubles would spread across the Irish Sea, causing violent deaths to many innocent people. I was invited to participate in a debate in Stirling University, my speech advocating the disbandment of the B-Specials. The votes went against me. I was once questioned at Stranraer harbour by a special branch officer while travelling by myself to Belfast from Stirling for a trip home. He quizzed me at length and examined my wallet and luggage but fortunately allowed me to board the ferry in time for me to continue my journey home.

On occasion, a large number of Queen's students participated in PD marches. But not all students supported the civil rights demonstrations; Protestant students were in the majority in the university, many of them were Unionists and most of them were perhaps loyalists. Paisley and supporters were active in the university, and set up the Ulster Constitution Defence Committee in May 1966.[30] A student branch of the DUP was formed in the university in 1971 with Jim Allister as first chairman, (he is at present leader of Traditional Unionist Voice, a rival unionist party to the UU and DUP).[31] The branch, comprising some thirty members, confronted Republican students and organised election campaigns to remove Republicans from office in the Students' Representative Council.

Lecturers with political connections were murdered. Miriam Daly, a lecturer in economic history, member of Sinn Féin and NICRA and active in prisoners' welfare, was murdered in her home by members of the Ulster Defence Association in 1980. Edgar Graham, lecturer in law and a Unionist Assembly member at Stormont, was murdered by the Provisional IRA in 1983.

Many Protestant students reported feeling ill at ease in the university. This can be viewed in the context of demographic changes in the composition of the student body. From 1960 to 1972, the undergraduate population almost doubled while the proportion of Catholics in a single year grew by 10%. This was part of a long-term trend. The proportion of Catholics in 1907-1908, when the university became independent, was fewer than 6% and had reached 50% by the end of the 1980s.[32] Queen's was no longer a predominantly Protestant university. Recent data from 2018-2019 show that 49.5% of students at Queen's and Ulster Universities are Catholic, compared to 31.2% Protestant and 19.3% 'other' ('O'Leary, p. 334).

One of my closest friends, who graduated two years after I did, recently shared the following reminiscences with me, fifty years after the event. His experience strikes a chord with my own: awareness of the political activity in the Student's Union, nevertheless a preoccupation with academic study when the examinations approached. Both of us, along with our friend Michael, left Northern Ireland after university and never lived there again; this pattern of Protestant emigration became increasingly common during the years of the 'troubles' (O' Leary, p. 15.)

My recollections of the political changes start in October 68 when I remember Michael coming back from a march in Derry where the water cannons were used and he told us all about it in the bar. And I have a memory of a People's Democracy march setting off from the Student Union Building. And I would try to spot the Special Branch men standing on the pavement. I recall that there were Catholic students in my class of 50 or so but I did not have much interaction with them. So, I can't really say if there was a cooling of relations as the political activity intensified. Strangely, though, I must have got into conversation with some of them at a dinner after the final exams in May of 1970 because I remember they took me to Ballymurphy to see the places where the trouble had occurred. In August 1969 I was working in London and remember reading about the trouble. Then I travelled in Europe for three weeks in September and came back for my final year in October. That year was work, work, work all the way through to the exams in May 1970 … I was so busy with the academic work that I did not pay much attention to the politics of it all. I do remember Terence O'Neill on television in late 1968 asking what kind of Ulster did we want - 'Ulster stands at the crossroads' was the phrase. And I remember the water was off for a while because of a bombing. We left our house in Suffolk [a Protestant housing estate in west Belfast, which has an interface with the Catholic Lenadoon estate] in December 1968 and moved to Finaghy, which was relatively peaceful. That was a very fortunate move because things got very bad in Suffolk in 69 and 70. It does all seem so very long ago now.

After the sixties

The political situation rapidly deteriorated from the riots of the late 1960s, and the death count of the Troubles rose inexorably, eventually passing 3,600 deaths by the 1990s. The causes of this have been extensively analysed, for example in the Cameron Report and books by Henry Patterson and McKittrick and McVea. In hindsight, a number of short-term factors were influential: the civil rights marches that were approved by the authorities but were obstructed by Paisley and his followers, unchallenged by the same authorities; the failures of the RUC in managing these events, poorly led by the government; the Stormont government's unwillingness at every step to meet any of the Civil Rights movements' demands; the riots and shootings that accompanied and followed the marches; the decision to send the British army into Catholic areas to arrest and intern Republicans, in the process imprisoning many innocent people; the shootings of innocent bystanders by the paratroopers on 'Bloody Sunday' on January 13, 1972. But would changes in any of these actions in themselves have altered the course of history? The Provisional IRA became entrenched, a secretive, ruthless guerrilla force using intimidation, bombs and shootings in pursuit of their goals. With Protestant paramilitaries also active in random assassinations of Catholics, Northern Ireland descended into a nightmare that lasted for more than thirty years.

This touched almost every family, although some communities, notably the most deprived, suffered much more than their share. Yet few families were spared. One of my cousins was very seriously injured as a young man by a bomb attack that was targeted at a senior judge. He was fortunate to survive and was hospitalised for a long time; his injuries continue to affect him into his retirement. But the whole population was affected, not least by the constant anxiety about the unpredictability of bombings, the killing and torturing of innocent people, the destruction of business, hotels and bars.

I was aware too of the destruction of buildings and businesses that had played a part in my personal life and in family occasions: The Red Lion bar on the Ormeau Road, blown up in 1971; Abercorn Restaurant (1972); Russell Court Hotel (1974 and again in 1976); Malone House (1976); La Mon Hotel (1978).

I acknowledge that I was living in Scotland, England and Wales from 1968 onwards so my experience bears little resemblance to those who lived in Northern Ireland. Nevertheless, I was not unaffected, anxious about my family, worried about the injuries suffered by my cousin and about my brother whose work took him travelling around Belfast on a daily basis. I made frequent visits home, particularly between 1968 and 1972 when I had student vacations so I had some personal experiences of the conflict. In August 1969, I was in Belfast during the five days of riots that brought the army in, and with my friend Jeff went behind the barricades on the Falls Road into 'Free Belfast' – an unsettling and nerve-wrecking experience. I was nervous that I might be recognised as a Protestant. The whole experience was not something I could share with my family. It was so strange to walk behind the makeshift barrier and to view the police and army from the other side. Would they stop me and question me when I came out again?

In 1973, I once accompanied my father to queue at a private house to buy milk during the Ulster Workers' Council's strike, the only means available to the farmers to get their milk to customers. The strike, a protest against the Sunningdale Agreement to introduce power sharing at Stormont, was led by loyalists in conjunction with paramilitaries from the UDA and UVF and succeeded in closing major industries and controlling the electricity supply. It brought about the resignation of Brian Faulkner as Chief Executive and the collapse of power-sharing in the Assembly. Intimidation by paramilitaries played a part but there was widespread hostility among the unionist community directed at Sunningdale.

When Sandra, on her first visit to the city centre, and I were travelling on a bus in Donegall Place, she was disconcerted when an armed squad of army soldiers boarded and walked up and down the bus, staring at everyone. I drove my father's car into the city centre in 1985, around the time of his funeral, and I was stopped at a barrier and questioned and was required to show documents at the army checkpoint followed by a brief search of the car. On another occasion, I was in a butcher's shop on the Cregagh Road waiting in a long line of customers to buy meat for my mother when a young man entered, marched straight to the front of the queue, ordered a large quantity of steaks and left without offering to pay. Nobody protested or even spoke while he was there or even after he left. He was a loyalist paramilitary. However startled we were by these events, it was everyday life for the city's residents including my family.

Eimar O'Callaghan's 1972 diary records her daily life in that year when she was sixteen, living in Andersonstown and attending St Dominic's Grammar School on the Falls Road. She heard explosions every night, gunshot most nights, and news about deaths most nights. She was kept awake by helicopters overhead, their noise and the searchlights that flooded her bedroom with light. She was also awakened by the noise of clashing metal bin lids alerting the residents to imminent army raids. Members of her family were frequently stopped and questioned at army checkpoints and roadblocks. The army was often in her street and one occasion a Saracen crashed into a parked car and drove off. The sounds of gun fire, explosions, helicopters hovering above, were daily occurrences.

She took the bus to school but services were frequently cancelled due to funerals on their way to Milltown Cemetery or because of stone throwing, rioting and the risk of hijacking and bus burning. An alternative, private form of transport was reliance on the former London Hackney cabs that ferried people up and down the Falls Road. (When I was a visiting lecturer for a few days at St Mary's University College, I used these cabs to travel between the college and my hotel in the city centre, sharing with as many passengers as could be squeezed in. There were no official stops; you told the driver where you wanted off.) Eimar O'Callaghan notes that she never visited other parts of the city other than occasional trips to the city centre.

She also describes the night after 'Bloody Sunday' in Derry when she lay awake in the dark – her father had insisted that there were no lights on upstairs because there were soldiers everywhere and they might be 'jittery'. She listened to the gunfire, the ambulances and fire engines, the helicopters overhead. She peeped out of the side of the curtain to see fires blazing. All the students were sent home the next day: 'at the hospital, a highjacked lorry was in flames, so was Falls Road Co-op and the Broadway cinema'.

After the Good Friday Agreement
After several unsuccessful attempts at reaching agreement, the Good Friday or Belfast Agreement was signed on April 10, 1998, following intense negotiations involving the Prime Minister Tony Blair and members of the British Labour government, representatives of the Irish and American governments and the EU, Sinn Féin, and members of the Stormont parliament, but not Paisley's DUP, which refused to take part. David Trimble of the Ulster Unionist Party and John Hume of the Social Democratic and Labour Party (SDLP) made significant positive contributions, as did President Clinton and US Senator George Mitchell. The Agreement was endorsed by referenda North and South of the border and ratified in international law.

Nevertheless, partition remains a live, divisive issue today even though in a plebiscite following the Good Friday Agreement, 96 percent of the Irish population endorsed its government's proposal to repeal the constitutional articles that claimed the six north-eastern counties as part of the Republic. A united Ireland remains an aspiration for a significant minority in Northern Ireland. Historically, Ulster Unionists (UU) used the threat of a united Ireland to frighten Protestant voters in elections, in part to head off any opposition from the labour or trade union movements. This fear was prominent in the 1960s when the Northern Ireland Labour Party began to make inroads into the Ulster

Unionist votes and there was concern among the latter's leadership that a Labour-Nationalist coalition might remove them from office and threaten the existence of the border. Unlike the rest of the United Kingdom, the Northern Ireland Labour Party has remained tiny and has won few seats at Stormont, even against a continuing background of low wages, job insecurity and consistently high unemployment.

The Troubles also strengthened partition *within* Belfast, with the erection of the 'peace lines' and 'peace walls' separating Protestant and Catholic neighbourhoods. These resulted in part from population movements across the city, when families were burnt out of their homes and were forced to relocate to safer areas among their co-religionists.

Inevitably, given the intransigence of different positions within Northern Ireland, the Good Friday Agreement was a hotchpotch of checks and balances, of giving vetoes to political parties that represented one or other side of the divide between unionists and nationalists. In effect, it legislated for the continuing existence of loyalist and nationalist parties, which was unavoidable at the time but has had the result of building an element of sectarianism into the constitutional structure. Sinn Féin and the DUP benefited most from the Agreement whereas Trimble's Ulster Unionists and Hume's SDLP, who had contributed much to the negotiations, were soon reduced to minority parties in the new Assembly. For lengthy periods since then, the Assembly has been suspended because of irreconcilable differences between the DUP and Sinn Féin, resulting in direct rule from Westminster.

A column by Noel Whelan in the *Irish Times*, September 19, 2014, titled, 'North still 'caught in the grip of sectarianism', describes the suspension of the Assembly in that year. The title of his article is taken from a public lecture given by Nuala O'Loan, the former Police Ombudsman of Northern Ireland, who took as an example of how the parties could not even agree to build a new, major stadium on the site of the now defunct Maze prison, rather than develop Ravenhill, Windsor Park and Casement Park. She adds that scarcely any significant legislation or important budgets have been passed by the Assembly.

Currently (April 2023), the Assembly is suspended yet again because of the DUP's refusal to elect a Speaker in protest over the Northern Ireland Protocol, a key element in the exit negotiations between London and the EU. The DUP was instrumental in bringing this impasse about when it briefly held the balance of power in the House of Commons during the Brexit debates. Rather than support the deal proposed by Prime Minister Theresa May it backed the more extreme positions advocated by Boris Johnson. That version of Brexit was incompatible with the Good Friday Agreement and has led to the prospect of a 'border in the Irish Sea', which is fiercely opposed by the DUP. This matter remains unresolved as I write; the DUP has rejected the Windsor Framework, an agreement negotiated between the UK and the EU in March 2023. Its MPs at Westminster voted against it in parliament on 22 March. It was passed by 515 votes to 29. Former prime ministers Johnson and Truss voted against it along with 20 conservative MPs. Despite this democratic endorsement the DUP blocked the Assembly from reconvening.

Britain's exit from the single European market and Customs Union has threatened the Agreement and harmed the whole of Ireland economically, socially and culturally. No leadership in the main Westminster political parties is prepared to acknowledge this, as I write. The DUP and Protestant paramilitary organisations remain stridently opposed to any changes that threaten the existence of the border. To them, it is a matter of principle. However, successive Conservative prime ministers act as though it can be resolved by bureaucratic changes. On their part, Conservatives regard the removal of the involvement of European courts in British affairs as a matter of principle. It is difficult to see how a political 'fudge' can resolve all of this.

Loyalists have experienced a series of crises in confidence that include the economic decline of the industrial North East and the growth in the service sector, for which increasingly well-educated Catholics are now qualified and competitive. Fair employment legislation has also helped Catholics make progress in the jobs market. Unionists have also observed the growth of the economy south of the border, in large part due to it being an English-language member of the EU, where, Andy Pollack writes, on several indices the standard of living is higher than that in the North. The years of population decline through emigration and an economy close to collapse due to protection policies advocated by De Valera are (one hopes) gone and Ireland is are no longer the poor relation to be looked down upon.

At the same time, the support of the British government, particularly a Conservative government, traditionally an ally of unionism, no longer appears so reliable to many loyalists. A series of public statements by British leaders illustrates this. In 1981, Margaret Thatcher asserted in a speech in her Finchley constituency that 'Northern Ireland is part of the United Kingdom; as much as my constituency is'. However, one of her ministers, Peter Brook, said that 'Britain has no selfish strategic or economic interest' in Northern Ireland, not something I presume he would have said of Finchley or Falkirk or Ferndale. The Downing Street Declaration of 1993 stated that 'it is for the people of Ireland, North and South, to achieve agreement without outside impediment. The British Government ... will encourage, enable and facilitate such agreement, and that they will endorse whatever agreement emerges and take the necessary steps to implement it'.

Also, it is clear from the Brexit deal negotiated by Boris Johnson's government that the implications for Northern Ireland were far from its priority and the DUP was misled about its implications for the border. Brexit was driven by English nationalism, not a United Kingdom-wide version. I cannot envisage a settlement with the EU that would affect a part of England in the same way that it impacts on Northern Ireland. English Conservatives are adamant that Scotland will be denied independence although many in Scotland would, I guess, welcome the opportunity to be in both UK and EU that is extended to Northern Ireland. Many loyalists are wary of relying on Westminster's good faith and perhaps have good reasons for doing so.

Despite its shortcomings, the Agreement has transformed Northern Ireland for the better. Thankfully, levels of violence have decreased markedly, although the threat persists. Individuals and families are still driven out of their homes and neighbourhoods. The paramilitary organisations on both sides have turned to crime, particularly the illegal drugs trade, cross-border smuggling and protection rackets.

A significant development since 1989 has been demographic, as described earlier. For the first time, the 2021census data show that the population of self-identified Catholics outnumbers that of self-identified Protestants (45.7% to 43.48%). The difference is small but the trend is a long-term one and is likely to continue: 1921 enrolment data for primary schools shows equal numbers of Protestant and Catholic children enrolled (46% in each case). O'Leary (p 15) suggests that one factor in this trend is the reduction in numbers of Catholics emigrating from Northern Ireland. Nevertheless, despite speculation in the media and among certain political commentators, this trend does not in itself mean a united Ireland is likely. An opinion poll in December 2022 conducted by *The Irish Times* and the Arins Research Project showed a large majority in Northern Ireland prepared to vote against a united Ireland, including 21% of Catholic respondents.

Nevertheless, the development poses a fresh dilemma for unionist parties, which will have to rely on unfamiliar methods of persuasion rather than intransigence or bullying to maintain the union with Great Britain. They also must adjust to the results in the most recent election, which meant that the leader of Sinn Féin would replace the DUP leader as First Minister in the Northern Ireland government once the Assembly resumes its business. There is also evidence of a slight but growing tendency among the younger electorate to move away from the extreme parties on either side to vote for middle of the road parties such as the Alliance Party. Changes lie ahead.

Queen's today

My alma mater has gone from strength to strength, has an international rather than a regional reputation and is now a member of the prestigious Russell Group of research-led British universities. There are more than 18,000 undergraduates. Since entry into the EU there has been an influx of students from the Republic. The image of the university has benefited from the Good Friday Agreement. Senator George Mitchell and Secretary of State Hillary Clinton, both advocates of the Agreement, have served as successive Chancellors of the University. The William J Clinton Leadership Institute was established in 2011, and the former President has been a frequent visitor. In 2022 a new Student Centre was erected on the site of the demolished Students Union that I knew and that had witnessed the protest marches and the formation of the People's Democracy.

The university is planning a conference to mark the 25th anniversary of the Agreement and the Clintons and Senator Mitchell are expected to attend.

Football after Queen's

When I arrived at Stirling University in September 1968 for my twelve-month Masters course, I promptly joined the football club. It was only the second year of the university's existence – its first cohort of 164 undergraduates and 31 postgraduates had started the previous year in September 1967 – so the numbers available for the football team were very small. The club fielded one side and later in the season raised a second side, and I played for the first team throughout the season against teams from other universities and colleges in Scotland. This was a very enjoyable experience.

The side was composed of undergraduates and postgraduates and we had some excellent footballers. We played our home matches in Bridge of Allan. I made life-long friends in the year I spent in Stirling, including Rob Ranyard who also played for the team. Nowadays the university has some 14,000 students and the football team plays in the Lowland Football League along with Celtic B, Rangers B and long-established league clubs such as Berwick Rangers, Cowdenbeath and East Stirlingshire.

In June 2018 Sandra and I attended a 50th anniversary reunion of the postgraduates associated with the MSc course and doctoral research in mathematical psychology. It was wonderful to see old friends again and their partners, although we were all sad at losses, including Dr Ranald Macdonald, with whom I shared a flat in the Upper Craigs, who passed away in 2007.

In September 1969 I moved to Keele University in Staffordshire on a two-year Northern Ireland Studentship to study for a PhD. I had not visited the university prior to the move and I wasn't at all sure where it was. The heavily industrialised Potteries with the steel works were a shock after the beauties of the mountains surrounding Stirling, the castle on its rock and the ancient buildings in the heart of the old city. The campus is located adjacent to Keele village, on the outskirts of Newcastle-Under-Lyme, which itself abuts the city of Stoke-on-Trent. I played football for the two years I was a postgraduate there and represented two teams, the university football club and a postgraduate society, Keele Research Association (KRA).

I played for the university 3rd XI as a midfielder for two seasons, but one Wednesday in my second year I was substitute for the 2nd XI, waiting on the touchline hoping for an opportunity to come on and make my debut, when the 1st XI, playing on an adjacent pitch, lost a player through injury and the captain called me over to play at right back. Many of the team had no idea who I was. This was the highest level of football that I would ever play at again and I thoroughly enjoyed the experience and the captain said afterwards that I played well: the game was so structured and there was so much passing and positional play, that my role was clear.

Unfortunately, I was injured in a five-a-side game shortly afterwards and missed several weeks football training and playing. The training sessions were sometimes led by two members of the Stoke City staff, a full-back Alex Elder, who was from Lisburn in Northern Ireland and had represented Glentoran and Burnley prior to joining the Potters, and a coach, Alan A' Court, who had been a winger for Liverpool (and whose picture card was one of my boyhood indoors game 'stars'). KRA played against other college teams within the university and, beyond university football, in Division II of the North Staffordshire Sunday League. I also played in an indoors five-a-side league in the university, competing in the gymnasium in the evening. The late Gordon Banks, the Stoke and England World Cup winning goalkeeper, also played in the league, albeit never in goal, along with other Stoke players. We called our team Melchester Rovers after the Roy Race character from comics.

My two years at Keele provided in many ways my most sustained and fulfilling experiences of football. I looked forward to reading the university team sheets when they were posted on the noticeboard in the Students Union, the coach journeys to away matches at other universities, and the games themselves. (In one match at Leicester University, I managed to score both goals in a 1-1 draw.)   I also enjoyed the training sessions, playing for KRA, the five-a-side league, and informal matches played in the gymnasium with friends including Colin Chant, John Piper and Dave Whitehead. We watched the 1970 world cup finals on television in the Students Union and cheered on the exceptional Brazil side that fielded Pelé at his peak – the goalkeeper, Felix, was a particular favourite of ours because of his error proneness and tendency to live dangerously. And threaten to undo the outstanding work of the talented outfielders.

We watched (what was at the time) First Division matches at Stoke City on a regular basis and travelled to away matches at Old Trafford, Maine Road, Manchester, Hillsborough in Sheffield, Wolverhampton, the Baseball ground in Derby, so that we saw the major players of the period.   I never intended to support Stoke City. I had gone to my first match because the away team was Tottenham Hotspur, with its associations with Danny Blanchflower, and in particular to watch Pat Jennings, then with Spurs. However, after a few more home matches I was a supporter. The club played at the Victoria Ground in Stoke-upon-Trent, one of the six towns of the Potteries that had merged in 1910. The old stadium – one of the oldest in the league – was opened in 1878 and was located among the terraced houses of Boothen Road and Lonsdale Road. It was showing its age.

Stoke had two outstanding sides in the 1970s under the management of Tony Waddington. The first was the one I followed regularly while I was at Keele, which won the League Cup in 1972 and reached the FA Cup semi-final in 1971, losing to Arsenal after a replay (I watched both matches). The second side included many of the same personnel in defence but was organised around the considerable talent of Alan Hudson, formerly of Chelsea, and with the England goalkeeper Peter Shilton replacing the retired Gordan Banks. The team challenged strongly for the First Division championship, finishing in fifth place in successive seasons having been top or near the top right up to the end of the season; in one week in the 1974-75 season, Liverpool, Everton, Stoke City and Derby County all had 47 points and were at the top of the First Division, separated only by goal difference.

However, the roof of the Butler Street grandstand was blown down in a gale in 1976 and the club was forced to sell its best players including Hudson and Shilton, to meet the costs of replacing it. The club vacated the Victoria Ground in 1997 and moved to a newly built stadium in the outskirts of Newcastle-under-Lyme.

The year 1972 was special for me. In April I obtained my first full-time job as a lecturer in Cardiff and I worked there from 1972 to 1983. In August Sandra and I married in Norwich, we moved to Cardiff and she started a teacher training course in Barry, qualifying in 1975 and taking up a teaching post in the town. I finished writing my PhD thesis in the same year.

I did not play any organised football during my time in Cardiff. I did have the opportunity to watch international matches at Ninian Park and to watch Cardiff City home games, particularly Stoke City whenever they were the visiting side. I never formed an attachment to the Bluebirds as I did with Stoke City and would do again with Preston North End. I suspect the regularity of attendance was a factor as well as going to matches at Stoke with university friends and with my son John at Preston. This would be consistent with the psychological theory proposed by Robert Zajonc that exposure in itself can increase liking for something.

Our children John and Beth were born in 1979 and 1982 respectively, and in 1983 I took up a lectureship in Preston and we relocated to Penwortham the following year. I began to play in an outdoor, evening, five-a-side league for men aged 35 years and over. We were mainly a team of teachers and called ourselves Academicals after the Scottish league side, Hamilton Academicals. We were put in touch with Mike Elwiss, who had been Preston North End's record signing at £70,000 in 1974 and was Alex Bruce's strike partner until he joined Crystal Palace for £200,000 before he was forced to retire through injury at the age of 27. We were short of a member and Mike joined us, but we struggled to keep up with him. He was physically very robust so it was good to have him on our side rather than as an opponent. I'm sure he found us exasperating, always urging us to close down our opponents' attackers. The coordinator of these leagues at Penwortham Leisure Centre was Alex Bruce, previously Preston North End's leading goalscorer in eight out of 10 seasons, 157 goals in all, who had played alongside Elwiss with PNE, and I got to know him quite well. He was friendly and very supportive of our team's efforts.

We had other connections with Preston North End. We discovered from our elderly neighbour that our house had once belonged to the football club and had been occupied by the manager, Cliff Britton, a former Everton and England player, who managed the club between 1956 and 1961. We imagined that the club legend, Sir Tom Finney, who spent his entire football career at Preston North End, must surely have visited our house. I had the privilege of having a conversation with Sir Tom at a presentation in the Harris Museum, and I was able to share with him that I had watched him play when he came out of retirement to play for Distillery in a European tie against Benfica in Belfast on September 25, 1963. He was 41 years of age at the time, nevertheless he was one of the best players on the pitch that night, even with the great Eusébio in the Portuguese side. The score was 3-3 (Distillery without Finney lost the return leg 5-0). Sir Tom was approachable and charming and clearly amused to be reminded of his first match for any team other than Preston and England. Sadly, he died in 2014 and the whole city came out to honour him.

Preston decided to replace their grass pitch with an artificial surface and sold off the turf to the public. I managed to purchase a square for our garden – unfortunately the turf along the wings where Finney had plied his trade was already snapped up. We organised a birthday party for our son John at the ground where we played a match under floodlights involving his sister and their friends, both boys and girls, and Sandra and our good friend, Val, served an *al fresco* birthday tea at the touchline.

John and I attended the club's home matches at Deepdale on a regular basis. We went one Saturday to watch the reserves play Liverpool reserves and found ourselves sitting next to Steve Heighway, the Liverpool and Republic of Ireland star, and managed to have a short chat with him. His team mate at the Merseyside club had been Brian Hall, who was now with Preston Council and we got to know him too through Sandra, who was working with the Council's youth programme.

In 1987 Preston signed a very talented young Irish winger Brian Mooney from Liverpool – like Terry Conroy, he had started with Home Farm in Dublin – and he remains one of the most exciting footballers I have ever seen. Helped by the artificial pitch, his dribbling skills turned opponents' defences inside out. He was a joy to watch. Tom Finney was an admirer of his skills. He was signed by Sunderland but he never again reached the heights he had achieved at Deepdale. After we moved back to Cardiff and John was training one evening at the Wales Sports Centre in the city centre, I slipped away to watch part of a match between the League of Ireland and the Welsh League that was taking place at the Athletics Stadium in the suburb of Leckwith. To my pleasant surprise, playing for the Irish side was the familiar figure of Brian Mooney, skilful as ever.

I was reminded of the ability of football to make connections many years later in 2012 when I spent a semester as a visiting professor at the University of Maryland College Park, which is located on the outskirts of Washington DC. I commuted to and from my lodgings in a university bus, and on my return trips in the autumn and winter evenings I came to know two Brazilian graduate students, Denis and Adriana, who were studying at Maryland. His spoken English wasn't too good, but when I told them that I was from Cardiff in Wales, he exclaimed 'Wales! Pelé scored against you when we beat you 1-0 in the World Cup'. I explained to them my interest in the 1958 World Cup finals and whenever we met on campus he would call out 'Pelé!' Their company was welcome on those bus journeys home through the dark evenings. I'm sure they are as saddened as I am by the great footballer's death in December 2022.

PART TWO: Bridging the Sectarian Divide

Segregation by residence

Some districts within Belfast and Londonderry/Derry, particularly in inner-city areas, have been segregated by religion since long before the foundation of Northern Ireland. The riots of the 1920s reinforced this, as did the events on August 15, 1969 when the RUC pursued Catholic rioters into the Catholic Bogside area and were followed by loyalist crowds attacking individuals and setting fire to properties. The rioting spread to Belfast later the same day, with loyalists attacking the Ardoyne and Crumlin Road areas of north Belfast and the Falls Road area in the west of the city and setting fire to houses, notably in Bombay Street, off the Falls Road. Catholic families were forced to flee their homes; McKittrick and McVea give the number of families displaced at 1,800 (1,500 of them Catholic). Residents set up improvised barriers, the forerunners of today's peace walls. There are now some 80 of these barriers in Northern Ireland.

People who grow up in Belfast acquire a mental map of the whereabouts of the Catholic and Protestant areas and where the boundaries between them lie. This is true of both private and public housing. Geographers produce maps depicting by means of colour coding the divisions within the city.

It is possible to quantify the degree of segregation through statistical analysis of census data. One approach, adopted by Paul Doherty and Michael Poole from the University of Ulster, is to divide the urban area into units of specified dimensions; in their study referenced here, these are 100 metres square. These units will vary in population but remain constant in size of area over time, unlike wards or constituencies that vary over time. This permits examination of temporal changes in population. The census forms request people to specify their religion; not all do so, for a variety of reasons, nevertheless the question can yield useful information. Finally, one needs a measure of segregation and alternative methods have been developed, for instance, the Dissimilarity Index widely used in international research. The Index ranges in value from $D = 0$, where the proportion of different groups within a unit matches that in the population, to $D = 100$, where there is maximum imbalance within the unit. (See Appendix 3).

When this method is applied to Belfast census data from 1971, 1981 and 1991 in the study conducted by Doherty and Poole, we note interesting changes. First, there is an overall population decline of 17% between 1971 and 1991, a trend that is more marked in Protestant areas. People are moving out of the city into surrounding areas. Second, there is a marked variation across the city in the relative proportions of Catholics and Protestants. If one looks at the 1991 data, for example, 31% of Belfast's population is Catholic. However, the proportion of Catholics is 75% in Belfast West and 47% in the Inner City, whereas it is only 6% in Belfast East and 8% in Castlereagh, which comprises suburbs to the east of the city.

Third, these was a marked increase over time in the Dissimilarity Index, following 1971. The D values for the three census dates were 49.6, 57.7 and 60.2. (In comparison, these D values approach the values of 62 and 66 found in studies of racial segregation in the largest cities in the US in the 1990s.)

The 1971 census was taken in April of that year but the inter-community violence started in August following the government's introduction of internment without trial of Catholics whom it believed were terrorists. During that summer more than 8,000 people were forced out of their dwellings.

Doherty and Poole applied a similar analysis to earlier censuses, albeit of ward information rather than physical units, from 1901 to 1971, and identified a similar trend, where there was a significant increase in segregation between 1911 and 1926, associated with the street violence of the 1920s. Residents are driven out of their home areas or else they move into safer areas to protect themselves from attack. Once again, specific areas, particularly the west of Belfast and inner-city Derry, bore the brunt of this. Doherty and Poole concluded (p. 528) that 'both the average Catholic and the average Protestant...live in an urban environment dominated by his or her ethnic group'.

Belfast South, where I lived and attended both primary and grammar schools and also university, saw a significant increase in the Catholic population, almost doubling from 17% in 1971 to 32% in 1991. What the census analysis can't show, unfortunately, is who relocated from one district to another, and why. Is the increase in Belfast South due to the increases in educational qualifications and employment opportunities among Catholics, enabling them to leave their predominately working-class heartlands for the petit bourgeois and middle class in the south of the city? Is this trend greater than an equivalent trend among the Protestant population? How are the findings affected by the methodology? For example, how are the boundaries between the parts of the city drawn up? Is the Protestant district of Sandy Row classed as Inner City or as belonging to Belfast West? Are the football stadium Windsor Park and its surrounding streets in Belfast West or South?

Population movements are complicated, influenced by many factors: demolition and redevelopment in inner-city districts; new developments including the construction of housing estates in the suburbs as the city expands its boundaries; the impact of the decline in industries and their sites in east Belfast; the 'gentrification' of hitherto working-class areas; increases in home ownership. Yet segregation in parts of Belfast is large by any standards and, as Doherty and Poole point out, is comparable to urban segregation on the basis of colour in the United States.

Segregation in public housing persists today. Public housing is extensive. In 2022, 27% of the population in Northern Ireland lived in accommodation provided by the Northern Ireland Housing Executive. According to the Executive, 94% of public housing in Belfast was divided on the basis of religious background in 2016 [33]. The Executive has attempted to address this, for example through programmes such as the Community Cohesive Strategy and the Shared Futures Housing Strategy. One approach is to attempt to control the flying of flags and the display of other sectarian symbols within Executive projects. Another policy is to specify that no more than 70% of residents in any housing project should be from one religious community. However, majority residents can take it into their own hands to eject minority tenants by means of threats and intimidation.

Negotiating the city

When I read China Miéville's novel, *The City & The City* I was struck by its parallel with Belfast. In the novel, the two cities, Besel and Ul Qoma, occupy adjacent geographical space, nevertheless exist as separate communities, each with its own culture and language. If you find your attention accidentally drawn to the other city, you must 'unsee' anything that is happening there. A 'cross hatch' is a zone where citizens of both cities can co-exist although 'unseeing' one another. Failure to obey the rules about segregation is severely punished by The Breach, a shadowy organisation responsible to the Oversight Committee, which is based in Cupola Hall. Uniquely, this building is located in both cities; it also provides the only border post where a citizen from one city armed with the correct documents can officially cross into the other. While they are there, they must learn see what had hitherto been unseen and to unlearn what they were used to seeing.

The novel reminds me of my own learning to navigate the segregated areas of Belfast. Citizens of these areas only mingled with their counterparts in other areas within the city centre. They shopped in the same department stores: Anderson & McAuley, Robinson & Cleaver, Robb's, the Co-op; they frequented the Gramophone Shop, Sammy Moore's Athletic Stores and Mullan's bookshop. They had tea and cakes in the Abercorn, and frequented the Opera House, the downtown cinemas, the bars, the dance halls. There was a wide choice of places to dance: the Plaza, Fiesta, Romanos, Betty Staff's, Sammy

Houston's, the Boom Boom Room. They celebrated each New Year at the Albert Clock. They paid their rates in the City Hall.

In the city centre, Protestants and Catholics were largely indistinguishable. I once went on a date with a girl I met in one of the dance halls; we arranged to meet outside Anderson & McCauley's but when I learned that Colette lived on the Falls Road I was reluctant to walk her home, she seemed relieved, and we parted amicably in College Square.

I gradually familiarised myself with the layout of the city, learning to distinguish safe and rough areas and to identify Protestant and Catholic districts and the boundaries between them. Our stretch of Ormeau Road together with the streets leading off it were largely Protestant and relatively safe although there were hard men and their gangs in the area often looking for trouble. When we headed downtown and crossed the Ormeau Bridge over the Lagan and passed the Apollo cinema, the streets to the left formed the district nicknamed the Holy Land, after the names of the streets, Damascus, Jerusalem, Palestine, Cairo, and so on. This was a respectable working-class area that I walked daily between my home and Queen's. In recent years it has become notorious for late-night partying and rubbish in the streets by the students who now form a substantial proportion of its population. The police are regularly called in, including having to respond to rioting on St Patrick's Day.

On the opposite side of the Ormeau Road is a group of streets between the road and the river – Hatfield and Farnham streets, and Balfour Avenue. I believe that it was a mixed area in the 1960s, because I knew

Protestant families who lived there and who attended our church or my primary school, but after the sixties it became Catholic and an area for Protestants to wary of.

Continuing along the main road towards the city centre you passed (or used to, before it was developed as housing) the North of Ireland Ormeau cricket and rugby ground. This was founded in 1859, and hosted cricket and rugby internationals over the years but its last match was played in 2001. Following a series of sectarian arson attacks and the burning of its pavilion – the club was seen by many as a bastion of Protestantism in what was by then a largely Catholic district – the cricket and rugby clubs relocated and the ground was sold for housing development. Opposite the ground stands Ormeau Road Methodist Church, built in 1873, which my parents attended, and which has since become an apartment block. Next, we would have passed what was then the gasworks, and now the area became rougher. After that was the end of Donegall Pass and Ormeau Avenue and the beginning of Cromac Street. The maze of small streets leading off to the right forms the markets area, traditionally a Catholic area that became a hotbed of Republican activity throughout the Troubles. At the end of Cromac Street is Cromac Square, site of one of the confrontations between Paisleyites and residents of the markets in the 1960s.

South of North Parade there are churches of the major denominations. On the Ormeau Road are Cooke Centenary Presbyterian Church, St Jude's Parish Church (Anglican) and Ballynafeigh Methodist Church. There is also Ballynafeigh Orange Hall. At the top of the Ormeau Road were the Convent of the Good Shepherd, and the Lys Marie Convent. There was a cluster of Catholic institutions on the Ravenhill Road that are now called St Michael's Primary School, St Joseph's College and Aquinas Diocesan Grammar School. Nazareth Lodge has also been a home for boys. This concentration of institutions is a further example of the importance of organised religion in the life of the city. As was the fact that shops on the Ormeau Road were closed on Sundays so we bought the papers from a temporary stand outside the bakery, braving the disapproval of churchgoers at Cooke Presbyterian Church opposite.

The east of the city on the other side of the river Lagan was then and remains solidly Protestant, with the exception of Short Strand, a small, isolated Catholic enclave immediately across the Albert Bridge. East Belfast was the location of the shipyard, the aircraft company, Short Brothers and Harland, the ropeworks and the Sirocco works. The clusters of streets of small terraced houses leading off the Newtownards Road were where many of the workers in these industries lived. In contrast, as we have seen, the west of the city was largely Catholic, with the exception of the Protestant Shankill Road, and you had to negotiate the boundaries between the Shankill and the Falls Roads with their connecting maze of side streets.

I was less familiar with the geography of the north of the city although it too has its segregated areas and contested interfaces. For example, the Ardoyne area is predominantly Catholic. A Catholic primary school for girls in the area, the Holy Cross School, is located within a Protestant area and in 2001 and 2002 the children and their parents had to run a daily gauntlet of abuse, threats and missiles from Protestant protesters as they made their way to and from school. They needed protection from police in riot gear to walk between home and school, and images of these shocking scenes were broadcast across the world.

Segregation by employment

The civil rights movement campaigned against discrimination in employment in addition to discrimination in access to public housing. The two communities offer alternative explanations of differential rates in employment. Many Protestants contend that Catholics are workshy and prefer to exist on benefits. Yet at the same time they maintain that Catholics take jobs away from Protestants. In turn, Catholics may underestimate the numbers in employment or exaggerate the barriers they face. Segregation in employment did exist, notably in the shipyard, which was predominantly Protestant, particularly in the skilled trades that required the successful completion of apprenticeships. However, even this is disputed.

Relevant data began to be collected in the 1970s, following the greater interest taken in Northern Ireland affairs at Westminster. Research drew upon statistical analysis of census returns from 1971 onwards and was augmented from the 1990s by findings from the annual Labour Force Surveys (LFS). The 1971 census data showed that unemployment rates were 5.5% for Protestants and 13.8% for Catholics. In the 1981 Census the rates were 11.4% and 25.5% respectively. The LFS data from 1990 to 2001 show that unemployment rates were falling overall but that Catholics were consistently approximately twice as likely to be unemployed. (Osborne and Shuttleworth, p. 15).

The issue was addressed in the Fair Employment (Northern Ireland) Act of 1989. The legislation established a Fair Employment Tribunal for Northern Ireland with the aim of promoting equality of opportunity between persons of different religious beliefs. As part of this, it requires employers of at least eleven employees (covering some 70% of the working population) to monitor the composition of their workforce, which necessitates the collection of data from their employees. Specifically, it records whether the individual is from the Protestant community or the Roman Catholic community, or neither. The monitoring form does not require that the employee practises a religion, merely that they identify with one or other religious denomination. The monitoring data permit analyses of changes over time in differential rates of employment, although interpretation needs to consider implications of changes in the labour market over time, where there has been a decline in industries and in the public sector and an increase in the service sector.

In 1994 the emphasis was on equality within government departments – the public sector is a major employer in Northern Ireland, more so than in the rest of the United Kingdom: In 2001, more than one in three of the monitored full-time workforce was employed in the public sector. In 1998 the legislation was put on a statutory basis as part of the Good Friday Agreement. There has been little emphasis on targets or on sanctions in the hope that employers will take voluntary action.

I illustrate the degree of change relying on data collected from 1990 to 2001 presented by Raymond Russell. In 1990, the Catholic share of the monitored workforce was 34.9%; by 2001 it had increased to 39.5%. The degree of change could also be analysed in terms of the nature of occupations, based upon the Standard Occupational Classification. This shows that increases in the Catholic share were largest among managers and administrators (8.6%) and professional occupations (10.5%) and smallest among craft and skilled manual occupations (1.1%) and plant and machine operatives (1.6%) (Russell, pp. 26-28). The finding that the largest increase among those professions that require post-school academic qualifications might reflect the growth in the numbers of Catholics acquiring these qualifications. It might also reflect the 'brain drain', where Protestant grammar-school students cross the Irish Sea to attend university, many of whom do not return to live and work in Northern Ireland.

Thus, there is evidence of increasing employment opportunities for the Catholic population. This does not address the question whether there is increasing integration in the sense that Catholics and Protestants in the same workforce have equal opportunities for recruitment and promotion. One approach to analysing recruitment is to examine the number of employees from the minority community within a given workforce. Has the proportion increased since fair employment legislation was brought in? Data analyses by Christopher McCrudden, Robert Ford and Anthony Heath suggest that the proportions have increased over time, albeit gradually. Their study investigated potential differences between those employers who signed an agreement to undertake affirmative action and those who did not. The study concluded that among the former employers, there were significant declines in in the numbers of highly segregated firms and a gradual movement in the direction of greater integration.[34]

For example, the number of firms employing less than 25% of the minority community declined from 561 in 1990 to 484 in 2000, a decrease of 8%. Among those firms without an agreement, the decline was 10%. One can also investigate changes in the proportion of the minority community within a firm's workforce, for example looking at the proportion of Catholic employees. Again, considering firms that agreed to take affirmative action, the proportion of Catholics employed within predominantly Catholic firms declined from 78.8% to 76.9%. Among predominantly Protestant firms the proportion of Catholics increased from 17.5% to 21.7%. Once more, the changes are in the desired direction but progress is slow.

Where fair employment is concerned, we ought to go beyond the global statistics and investigate whether there are equal opportunities for promotion within a firm and whether there is potential for career development. For example, employment as night-time office cleaners, posts often occupied by women from ethnic minorities, offers little scope for advancement and hence can give a misleading impression of the degree of integration in that firm. There are avenues here for future research.

The findings I summarise here are only illustrative: There is not scope here to do justice to the wealth of data that has been reported and continues to emerge since 1990 or to bring findings up to date. It is perhaps unsurprising that progress is slow, given the long history of inter-community hostility and violence along with segregation in housing in working-class areas –

the religious composition where one lives can influence employment opportunities in various ways. One conclusion to draw is that segregation and integration are now officially regarded as serious issues and steps are being taken to influence, monitor and publicise findings about these. The university sector has been active in analysing Equality Commission data and publishing its findings in peer-reviewed scientific journals that attest to the robustness of the findings.

The police service is a special case in several ways. Nationalists regularly complained that the Royal Ulster Constabulary (RUC) was predominantly Protestant, and evidence supports that view: Only 8% of officers was Catholic at the time of the Good Friday Agreement (GFA). The Patten Commission that accompanied the GFA recommended a specific target, namely of equality in recruitment (50:50, Catholic: Protestant) 'from the pool of qualified candidates'. This policy has been implemented in part since 2001 and the numbers of Catholic officers increased over the years to 32% of the force.

Nevertheless, there remains dispute about the extent to which the reforms set out in the Patten Report have been implemented by the Police Service of Northern Ireland (PSNI, the RUC's successor force). According to a report in the *Belfast Telegraph* in November 2021, the Deputy Chief Constable of the PSNI stated that it would take at least another ten years before the 50:50 target was reached. Another article in the same newspaper in March 2023 suggested that the recruitment policy had ended in 2011. A report issued by the PSNI, *Equality Scheme [Equality, Diversity and Good Relations Strategy, 2017-2022]* acknowledged the need to promote equality of opportunity including 'between persons of different religious beliefs [and] political opinions...' but was not more specific on the question of targets. The document set out a series of stages of implementation and monitoring from 2017 to 2022. Time will tell whether targets will be met.

Once again, we can speculate whether the conflict in Northern Ireland would have taken the form and duration it did if this kind of employment legislation and clear criteria for allocation of social housing had been in place in the 1950s and 1960s. I turn now to segregation in schooling.

Segregated school systems

Sport can contribute to reducing segregation and increasing inclusiveness. This claim was made during a conference in Wilton Park in 2022 hosted by the Northern Ireland Office and the UK Foreign, Commonwealth and Development Office when it turned its attention to children and young people. It argued that sport can increase social interactions and one proposal was that there should be greater sharing across schools in local areas as part of increased 'engagement between schools of different backgrounds on a regular basis.' Where the segregation of sports is important is in the sense that it keeps young people apart in an area of life that is significant for this age group, not only in active participation but also in terms of social identification.

Before discussing the various attempts to increase interpersonal contact between the communities, it is useful to introduce important differences in the organisation of the school systems north and south of the border and between Northern Ireland and England.

School education is a devolved matter in the United Kingdom, resulting in variation among its four constituent jurisdictions.

North and South

I begin with the role of the churches in the two education systems post-partition. The Catholic Church controlled the education system in the South. To illustrate, according to the historian Diarmaid Ferriter, in 1978 the Catholic Archbishop of Dublin was patron of 541 schools; between them, the Catholic bishops of Ireland were patrons of just under 3,000 schools. [35] The novelist John McGahern fell afoul of this, when he lost his teaching post following the Church's intervention after he had married in a registry office. He specifically blamed John McQuaid, Archbishop of Dublin and Primate of Ireland, for this decision; McQuaid had a record of involving himself in individual cases.[36] However, the influence of the Church on the management of schools began to diminish somewhat in the 1960s and 1970s. In the face of strident opposition from the Catholic hierarchy, the Education Act of 1998 enhanced the role of teachers, parents and community representatives in the management of schools.[37] Nevertheless, the Equal Status Act of 2000 allows schools to discriminate on religious grounds in their admission policy. The school leaving age was raised to 14 in 1926 and to 15 in 1947. Free secondary education lagged some twenty years behind Northern Ireland and was only introduced in September 1967.

Northern Ireland has two educational sectors, the controlled and the voluntary or maintained. The former is controlled and financed by the state through the Department of Education, via the Education Authority, set up in 2014, and school governing bodies. The maintained sector is also financed by the state and is managed by the Council for Catholic Maintained Schools (CCMS). It was set up in 1987 as a statutory body funded by the Department of Education, managing the sector though diocesan committees and school governing bodies. In reality, the former are Protestant schools and the latter, as the name of the CCMS suggests, Catholic schools.[38] It is important to note that parents and their children can choose to attend either controlled or maintained schools, thus they are not segregated in law. But in practice each school recruits from either a Protestants or a Catholic community.

This is confirmed by data collected over the years. Professor Cairns of the University of Ulster quoted results from a survey conducted in 1977, which reported that 90% of Catholic primary schools had no non-Catholic students and 67% of Protestant schools were solely Protestant. A similar degree of segregation was evident among teachers. Of the 2,751 teachers in the sample, only 41 taught in a school of the other religion. Another salient result from the survey was that the Irish language was widely taught in Catholic schools but not at all in Protestant schools.

Findings from 2005-2006 reported by Professor Gallagher of Queen's University in 2010 shows that the picture had scarcely changed since 1977: 4% of Catholic pupils attended Protestant schools; 1% of Protestants pupils attended a Catholic school. Another set of data, this time from a 2022 study reported by a team at Ulster University shows a similar picture. For grammar schools, the proportions attending school of the same religion was 66% for Protestants and 95% for

Catholics. For non-grammar schools the equivalent percentages were 75 and 94 (reported by Roulston).

It might be helpful to look briefly into the history of this. In 1921, the new Stormont government needed to set up from scratch an administrative infrastructure to support education and teacher training in the new jurisdiction. Existing British legislation prohibited the state endowment of any religious body so the government proposed that all schools should be nondenominational. However, this was strongly resisted by the churches. The Catholic Church would not relinquish its control of schools. Following strong protests against the proposed legislation, the Protestant churches negotiated with the government and obtained the right to nominate the majority of the school management committee and to exercise control over teacher appointments.

The opposition of the Catholic church to nondenominational education has been interpreted by some as demonstrating its unwillingness to fully recognise the constitutional status of Northern Ireland. Its counter-argument is that the religious basis of the Church's teaching would be diluted within a state system. As we have seen, the outcome has been that Protestant and Catholic children have with few exceptions attended different schools for one hundred years.

Nevertheless, there has been a slow movement away from segregation in both jurisdictions. In the South, there has been a gradual increase in the number of community and multidenominational schools including the Dalkey School Project, which was set up in Dun Laoghaire, just south of Dublin, where a group of parents initiated a multidenominational school. According to the school website in 2022, there are now 56 multidenominational schools in Ireland.

The North has also witnessed an increase in the number of students educated in nondenominational, 'integrated' schools. I return to this in a later section where I consider the merits of increasing contact between Catholic and Protestant school students. In summary, when we consider that the majority of schools in Northern Ireland are denominational and that there has always been a degree of segregation in housing in both private and public sectors, most children will grow up acquainted with and forming friendships with children of their own religion. This certainly was my experience in the 1950s and 1960s. Parents would have had a similar experience, and this segregation can, as we have seen, extend to the workplace and social and leisure activities in adulthood.

Differences in attainments

The secondary-level sector differs between jurisdictions. In Northern Ireland it is provided in either grammar schools or secondary schools. Admission to grammar school is by means of academic selection and the results of transfer tests are used to allocate places. The two types of secondary schools were introduced following the British Education Act of 1944, and the results from the Qualifying Examination at around age eleven years (widely known across the UK as the Eleven Plus) determined whether pupils qualified for a grammar school place or attended a non-selective school. (I recall walking from my school with the handful of my fellow pupils who were also entered for the Qualifying Examination to Botanic Primary School, where we were to sit it.)

The rest of the United Kingdom moved in the 1970s towards comprehensive secondary education without any selection process but it was not until 2008 that the Qualifying Examination was abolished in Northern Ireland. This step was resisted by the grammar schools, which responded by setting up their own admission tests, which are now run by two consortia, one for mainly Catholic schools and the other for mainly Protestant schools. Thus, selection for entry to grammar schools remains in place. Parents pay a fee for their children to sit the tests. It could be as high as £60 although the fee is waived for pupils eligible for free meals.

I was surprised by two aspects of this procedure. First, it seems unnecessarily divisive to have two consortia and thereby contribute to maintenance of the denominational difference. This is now changing and a single consortium – the Schools Entrance Assessment Group (SEAG) – was set up in February 2022 and the first tests will be administered in November 2023. The consortium's directors are principals of grammar schools. Second, grammar schools are funded by the state and I was surprised that they were allowed by the state to set up their own selection tests. Selection for post-primary schooling is surely an important matter for the state-run educational system because of its impact on children's life chances and ought not to be contracted out. Evidence shows that the qualifications that can increase a young person's social mobility are much more likely to be obtained in a grammar school setting than in the non-selective sector.

Another factor to consider is that there are two kinds of schools in the secondary sector – grammar and non-selective – but only one of these calls the shots over admissions. The grammar schools' policies and selection criteria have direct implications for the non-selective sector, which has little say in the matter. Thus, for example, an expansion in the grammar schools' numbers of admissions has budgetary implications for the other sector. Expansion of places also deprives that sector of able students who could act as role models for their peers. There are other matters to consider. A child's test performance might result in admission to grammar school in one year but the same performance might not do so in another year depending on marking criteria, even though his or her ability, aptitudes or preparation remain the same. Furthermore, many students begin their secondary education with a sense of already having failed.

The organisation south of the border is different. There are three types of secondary school: Voluntary (57% of the sector, mainly owned and managed by religious organisations, many fee-paying); Education and Training Board (ETB) (28%); Community Comprehensive (15%). All these secondary schools follow the same curriculum and qualifications framework. Following recent statutory change, secondary schools in Ireland are not allowed to assess students for admission.[39]

It is never straightforward to make comparisons among different educational systems, not least because of their variations in qualifications, but an Economic and Social Research Institute (ESRI) 2022 study identified differences between the North and the South in attainments and expectations in secondary education. Its approach was to identify a sample of a cohort of adults, aged from 25 to 29, and examine the highest educational qualifications obtained by each member of the sample.

The ESRI reports that 19% in Northern Ireland had the *lowest* attainments compared to 8% in Ireland. Conversely, a *higher* proportion in Northern Ireland is educated to upper secondary level (37% compared to 22%) These differences may be influenced by the selective system in the North, where proportionally more students had the lowest levels of attainments and were more likely to leave school earlier than their Southern counterparts. At the other end of the spectrum, a higher proportion in Ireland left education with post-secondary qualifications (30% compared to the North's 11%). There was no difference in proportions obtaining a degree or above.

There are also differences in measures of attainment between Northern Ireland and other regions of the United Kingdom. A report by Fact Check NI (November 23, 2022) confirmed findings that an average of 6.3% of young people across the nine regions of England for which data were available lacked educational qualifications. The comparable figure in Northern Ireland is 10.4%. However, the authors of the report argue that these statistics fail to take into account the 'brain drain' where only 36% of university students who have taken their degree outside Northern Ireland return after graduation, i.e., the data underestimates the numbers who have qualifications. They also claim that the ESRI report suggested that

Northern Ireland was not so discrepant from the rest of the UK. [40]

There is evidence of differences in academic performance *within* Northern Ireland between Catholic and Protestant schools, for example in data collected for the years 2007 and 2012. To take the latter date, the difference between Catholic and Protestant schools was 5% points in favour of Catholic schools in the numbers obtaining five and more 'good' GCSEs (graded A*-C), and their relative superiority was by 7.3 points at A-level. This difference was also reflected in post-school outcomes where Catholics were much more likely to go on to higher education whereas Protestants were more likely to enter job training. The 2015 report by Stephanie Burns and colleagues expressed concern about the lower educational attainments of males, particularly Protestant males.

A survey of school leavers' attainments in GCSE and A-level in the academic year 2013/2014 in Northern Ireland reported by Borooah and Knox showed that, overall, girls out performed boys and students from Catholic schools outperformed their Protestant contemporaries. The percentages obtaining 'good' GCSE results (grades A to C) were respectively 67.1% (girls) and 58.3% (boys); at A-level, 41.6% and 31.6%.

There was also a strong effect of the degree of multiple deprivations in the school's neighbourhood. If schools are divided into five groups on the basis of levels of deprivation, the most deprived areas' 'good' GCSE results were obtained by 53.5% whereas the equivalent for the least deprived neighbourhoods was 68%. The effect on performance in GCSE was most pronounced among those males who were entitled to free school meals, a frequent index of relative economic disadvantage in educational research. The data for 'good' A-levels were 28.9% for those entitled to free schools and 40.7% for the males who were not. [41] We should bear in mind that these differences are relative: substantial numbers of the most deprived students perform well at school despite their disadvantages.

Surveys of school 'league tables', i.e., tables listing the relative standing of schools across the United Kingdom on a number of relevant measures, support this picture. The *Sunday Times* table for 2022 included seven Northern Ireland schools in the top 50. Within Northern Ireland's 'top ten', Catholic schools occupied five places including the first three places (St Mary's Grammar School Magherafelt; Aquinas Diocesan Grammar School, Belfast; Our Lady and St Patrick's College, Belfast.)

In summary, the selective system in Northern Ireland is associated with strong performance by those obtaining the highest qualifications and weak performance among the lowest achievers. It is not clear why Catholic schools outperform Protestant schools north of the border and why Northern Ireland schools overall perform less well than schools south of the border, which are largely Catholic. Nevertheless, the low attainments within the non-grammar school sector in Northern Ireland remain a worry for economists and politicians, in the light of the long-term trend away from traditional manual forms of employment to the necessity of a more technologically skilled and adaptable workforce. This will continue to be an important issue, with the aim of attracting high-tech international companies to the region.

Increasing Interpersonal Contact

Theory and research

Anything that keeps groups apart increases the risk of prejudice and conflict. This assertion has been at the heart of the psychological study of prejudice, notably the theorising of Henri Tajfel, born into a Jewish family in Poland, a German prisoner-of-war during the Second World War, and who worked after the war with refugees before moving to Britain, where he became Professor of Social Psychology in Bristol University. He died in 1982, but his research continues to be developed by others and has been applied to Northern Ireland.

Tajfel's Social Identity Theory was strongly influenced by his personal experience in early life of discrimination and conflict. Central to his thesis is the natural human process of categorisation: we organise our social world into categories and make use of these to understand it and these in turn influence our actions. These can take the forms of prejudice, discrimination and hostility. We have encountered many examples of these throughout this essay: Protestant, Roman Catholic, Paisleyite, Ulster Unionist, republican, nationalist, communist, Trotskyist, and there are countless others: politician, immigrant, asylum seeker, Brexiteer, Jew, Palestinian. We use these categories to structure our everyday experience.

A group can be, but is not necessarily, an organised, structured or formal group like the DUP, NICRA or the Roman Catholic Church. There will be those who identify with the DUP's policies and actions but who are not members of the party. Indeed, they may not live in Northern Ireland or know any of its members personally. It functions as a group psychologically to the extent that people identify with it. We are all members of multiple groups in this sense. In Northern Ireland we can identify broad groups, 'protestant' and 'catholic', 'unionist' and 'nationalist' that have divided people for many years on the basis of religious and national identities.

This is how we categorise one another when we share information with someone, when we are introduced to someone or learn about them in the media. When we meet someone for the first time, an early question we pose ourselves is which group(s) they belong to (or which foot they kick with; 'left-footer' is often a synonym for Catholic). Where the religious categorisation is concerned, we make use of cues such as a person's name, the school they attended, where they live, perhaps their employment. The teenage Eimar O'Callaghan wished that had a name that is less associated with Irish Catholicism – 'I might as well have had the word 'Catholic' branded on my forehead', she writes in her diary. Anthropologists, for example, Rosemary Harris, call this judgment process 'telling'. Once we believe we have established to which group the person belongs, we make inferences about other aspects of their life and we can adjust our behaviour accordingly, perhaps steering clear of contentious topics.

Social identity can be fluid. It can be salient at some times and less so at others. My Protestant identity might become important to my social identity at one time but not at another. My social identity has implications for my sense of who I am and how I evaluate myself. I feel better about myself if I feel positive about the group I belong to or I feel superior to the group I don't belong to. I feel positive about myself when I participate in or witness ceremonies or events that give value to my group, for example watching the bonfire burning on the night before the 12th July and seeing effigies of hated members of the out-group going up in flames, or watching the procession of Orangemen the following day. One's social identity is not superficial and can exert a strong influence on behaviour, including discrimination and violence.

Tajfel's theory and the research it stimulates offer insights into how conflict between groups can be reduced. In particular, it emphasises the value of personal contact between members of different groups. Prejudice between groups can be reduced by bringing them together in the right circumstances, that is, when there is a positive social atmosphere and when their members participate in shared endeavours.

Contact with others can make us aware that members of the out-group are individuals and do not all share the qualities a stereotype attributes to them. We can learn that they are like us. It can help to reduce anxiety about interacting with people whom we imagine are unlike us. It can foster empathy with members of the out-group.[42] Research finds that people who have friends in the other community or who have greater contact with them are less prejudiced than those who do not have friends or who have fewer contacts.

Nevertheless, the circumstances of contact count, and close contact can have adverse effects, heightening aggression and conflict, as was the case at Burntollet Bridge or the rioting in Cromac Square, to take two examples. Anticipation of the potential risks of social interaction can create anxiety and a sense of threat. This can be realistic – the threat of physical violence, destruction of property, of loss of freedom. It can be symbolic, an attack on one's religion, one's sense of autonomy and one's values. There are many instances of symbolic threat in Northern Ireland: paramilitary displays, uniforms, Balaclava headwear, sunglasses, uniforms, national flags and weapons at funerals, bonfires, Lambeg drums, burning effigies, graffiti.

A series of research studies conducted in Northern Ireland has investigated the contributions of several factors to people's attitudes to members of other groups. These include the quality and quantity of contact between groups, the strength of an individual's identification with a group, their anxiety about other groups and their perception of threat. How do these affect attitudes to the religious out-group, for example, Protestant attitudes to Catholics? Degree and quality of contact with the other group among university students can be assessed by asking participants how much contact they have with members of the other community whether at meetings or events, when chatting to people, and in social situations in general.

Nicole Tausch and colleagues' study of Protestant and Catholic university students found that the higher the quality of contact, the less anxiety and feelings of symbolic and realistic threat were expressed. The more frequent the contact, the more positive the attitude to the other group. Similarly, the less anxiety and symbolic threat experienced, the more positive the attitude.

The relationship between perceiving symbolic threats to the in-group and attitude to the out-group was influenced by strength of identification with the in-group. For example, stronger identification with the

Orange Order would mean that the greater the perceived or imagined threat to the Order from outside, the more negative the attitude to Catholics.[43] Studies like these – and this is only one example – can tease out some of the factors involved in the nature of connections between contact and attitudes to the other community. Nevertheless, more robust studies would draw upon measures of actual contact rather than self-reported contact and they would study populations beyond university students.

Consciously attempting to influence contact between groups has been attempted in Northern Ireland. A longstanding project has been the Corrymeela Community, founded and initially led by Ray Davey, then a Presbyterian Dean of Residence at Queen's, a former prisoner of war in Dresden who experienced first-hand the bombing of the city. A site at the townland of Corrymeela near Ballycastle was purchased and a centre for peace and conciliation set up in 1965. It is still thriving today. Its mission is to 'Transform Division through Human Encounter' and it has organised conferences, educational programmes, workshops, and residential courses for young people. It hosts over 11,000 people a year. One problem with this approach is that attitudes are not simply properties of individuals but are shared in communities so that the young person who returns to his or her community can find their changed attitude a minority one and hence a challenge to their social relationships.

Contact through school
An alternative approach has been to work through the schools, whether through the curriculum or by increasing contact between pupils from Protestant and Catholic schools. Attempts at curricular development

include Education for Mutual Understanding (EMU), Cultural Heritage (CH) and Local and Global Citizenship, the last of these a timetabled subject, made compulsory in 2007. Gallagher (2010) suggests that increasing contact in this way has often proved difficult in practice, involving relatively few students or being restricted to safe and unchallenging topics.

Dirk Schubotz and Gillian Robinson report findings from surveys of sixteen-year-olds, the Young Life and Time survey (YLT), during the period 2003 to 2005, when most participants would have been exposed to EMU and CH. The survey showed that 42% who lived in predominantly Catholic areas and 32% who lived in predominately Protestant areas reported having no friends at all from the other religious community. However, the equivalent figure for those who lived in mixed neighbourhoods was 20%. The researchers also found that participation in cross-community events was related to more positive feelings towards the other community, although the most frequent answer was that it did not affect feelings. Five per cent of the sample attended integrated schools and these students showed a modest increase in positive feelings. Overall, few respondents to the survey (from 6% to 15%) reported having unfavourable feelings towards the other community.

The Shared Education Signature Project targeted at curriculum-based collaboration among schools was pilot tested in 2007 and put into practice with 25 million pounds funding from a private foundation, Atlantic Philanthropies, the Office of the First Minister and Deputy First Minister at Stormont, and the Northern Ireland Department of Education. A report to the Northern Ireland Assembly claimed that programmes had been taken up by 61% of Primary, Post Primary and Special Schools by 2019.[44] It overcomes some of the limitations identified by Gallagher in that is not an add-on to the curriculum but delivers through the curriculum. It extends the range of curricula and draws upon expertise from different schools. It emphasises collaboration among two or more schools but, unlike integrated schooling, described below, students retain the community identity of their own school.

In light of their analyses of factors influencing attainments at GCSE and A-levels, Borooah and Knox suggest that collaboration might also be designed to improve standards by, for example, pairing more successful with less successful schools. In terms of their findings, it might mean in theory pairing Catholic girls' schools in less deprived areas with Protestant boys' schools in the most deprived areas. This would aim to raise educational standards and reducing segregation at the same time.

Another approach is the formation of integrated schools, where children from both communities are taught within the same school. The notion that good relations will be more likely if children are educated alongside one another is not new. It preceded the foundation of Northern Ireland. In 1831 the government's intention was to set up a nondenominational educational structure in Ireland, but it encountered opposition from Catholic and Presbyterian churches in particular, which argued that education was an extension of pastoral care. In face of this opposition, which included a Presbyterian campaign that involved burning schools and intimidating teachers, the government retreated.

This issue arose again following the establishment of the Northern Ireland government at Stormont. The incoming government's preference was system was for nondenominational schools but once again, as we saw in an earlier section, opposition from the churches prevented this from happening. In 1924, the principal Protestant churches came together to form the United Education Committee and its campaign to avoid the secularisation of schools helped to ensure the dual system that has lasted to the present day.

An influential development was initiated in 1981 by Lagan College in Belfast, an integrated secondary school that has now more than 1500 students. The integrated schools movement obtained government encouragement for its development in the 1989 Education Reform Order. The Ministry of Education website (November 2022) reports that there are currently 70 grant-aided integrated schools, comprising 38 grant-maintained integrated schools (23 Primary and 15 Post-Primary) and 32 controlled integrated schools (24 Primary, six Post-Primary and 2 Nursery). This comprises 7% of Northern Ireland schools. However, the numbers of schools seem to have reached a plateau at this proportion.[45]

Nevertheless, attitudes among politicians in the Assembly have failed to keep in step with findings from opinion polls that show that a majority of parents are in favour of integrated education. A poll in May 2021 found that 73% of respondents favoured it and 71% favoured it becoming the mainstream.[46] A Private Member's Bill was brought before the Assembly by Alliance Party member Kellie Armstrong, and it completed its final reading on March 9, 2022. The DUP opposed the Bill, arguing that it would be to the detriment of the 93% of traditional schools. It was also opposed by the UU party and by organisations representing schools' management.

The DUP attempted to veto the bill by calling upon a procedure called Petition of Concern that is designed to avoid one community being outvoted by the other. Implementation of this needed the support of the UU, but this was not forthcoming, the UU arguing that the procedure was not designed for this purpose, it being a matter for democratic resolution. The Bill was passed by 49 to 38 votes and received Royal Assent on April 26, 2022. This places a statutory duty on the Department of Education to provide further support for the integrated schools sector, including setting minimum targets for the number of schools in the sector. Time will tell what impact this will have on the future of integrated schools.

Increasing interpersonal contact is not a panacea. While it can provide a valuable learning experience and help to change attitudes, an individual's attitudes are not idiosyncratic but are shared with the other members of the group they identify with and their community. To return to your group after a period of contact with an out-group can be challenging, since you might be out of step with the values of your in-group and might be forced to hide any genuine change. Attitudes serve social as well as personal functions.

Research into integration continues on different fronts, not only in terms of intergroup psychology but also in the areas of educational policy and organisational structures such as the management of the controlled and maintained sectors and the process of selection of students for grammar and secondary schools. There are research centres in the two major universities: Queen's University and the University of Ulster. The former hosts the Centre for Shared Education, set up in 2012, building on research studies dating back to 2007. The latter hosts the UNESCO Centre for Integrated Education, the first UNESCO Chair having been appointed in 1999.

The selective nature of the educational system might impact on the goals of shared education, as a 2022 paper by Joanne Hughes and Rebecca Loader of the Queen's University Centre argues. The relationship between the two might be relevant because of the long-established link between selection for grammar school and social class. Middle-class children are more likely to be admitted into grammar schools. This can be construed as an additional form of segregation. Children from deprived communities are less likely to gain admission into grammar schools, making it more difficult to obtain academic qualifications that might lift them out of their community and open up job markets to them. In turn, the community is more likely to be divided from their neighbours of the other denomination and susceptible to coming under the influence of paramilitary groups.

Hughes and Loader report results from a study of school leavers conducted by Borooah and Knox (2107) that found that high levels of segregation by religion was associated with higher achievement among Catholic pupils overall but lower achievement among Protestant boys in particular.

Nevertheless, the degree of popular support for integrated education and the increased likelihood of sharing educational experiences between the two communities through, for example, the Shared Education Signature Project shows possible ways to increase interpersonal contacts and break down unnecessary barriers. It will mean challenging some of the vested political and religious interests in Northern Ireland.

Eddie's Question revisited

The separation of sports with which I grew up and that provided the stimulus for this essay persists. Protestants continue to play a range of sports that excludes Gaelic games. Catholics, on the other hand, are willing to play and follow many sports, particularly soccer. Furthermore, following the professionalisation of rugby union, several players have moved from Gaelic football to become rugby internationals and have contributed to a successful Ireland team.

Newry-born Pat Jennings, the great Tottenham Hotspur, Arsenal and Northern Ireland goalkeeper (119 caps), played soccer as a boy for the Dublin side Shamrock Rovers, switched to Gaelic football from fourteen to sixteen years of age, after which he joined Newry, the local Irish League soccer club, before being transferred to Watford. He was taught at school in Newry by the future politician and deputy first minister of Northern Ireland, Seamus Mallon, himself a keen Gaelic footballer, who represented his village side, Mullaghbrack as well as St Joseph's Teacher Training College, where he trained to be teacher. Mallon also played for Middletown, Keady, Queen's University and Crossmaglen Rangers and represented Armagh at county level. He wrote in his autobiography about his early years at school and college, that 'my life was centred around football'.

John McGahern, the novelist and short-story writer followed Gaelic football and hurling and regularly attended the football cup finals at Croke Park. He also followed association football and when he lived in

London he regularly attended matches, for example, he and his girlfriend watched George Best, whom he greatly admired, play for Manchester United against West Ham United on September 2, 1967. After he returned to live in Ireland, he would watch the FA Cup final on television in a local bar.[47]

More recently, Niamh Marley, an experienced Gaelic footballer from a family of GAA sport participants, her father having played in the 1977 All-Ireland final, has represented Ulster at Rugby Union and played Gaelic football for her local club, Lissummon and at county level for County Armagh. Indeed, in January 2023 she played for Ulster on the Saturday and Armagh on the Sunday.[48]

The two football associations in Ireland remain distinct and the split in 1921 has never healed. Vague talks among players from north and south of the border, who are sometimes colleagues in the same English league teams, about the prospect of a united Ireland international team, and speculation about how strong a combined side would be remain only that. What does this stasis mean and does it relate to the problems that have beset Northern Ireland and remain unresolved? Or are they quite separate issues? Sport is perhaps a small matter in the grand scheme of things and its significance ought not to be exaggerated. Nevertheless, it plays an important part in many people's social identity, including their identification with particular clubs and national sides. This is particularly noticeable in a small country like Wales, where rugby and, more now, soccer, brings people together in a unique fashion. The crowd's singing of *Yma o Hyd*, written by Dafydd Iwan, during matches in the recent World Cup campaign provides a highly emotional experience.

I acknowledge that association football and its Gaelic counterpart have long been embedded within different cultures. The former has traditionally had its base in the urban working class, particularly in the industrial cities of Glasgow, Manchester and Liverpool. The coalfields of the North East and the Lancashire and Yorkshire mill towns have also had more than their share of successful clubs and outstanding individual players. In contrast, Gaelic is rural and agrarian, and its traditional heartland lies in the small parishes of the more agricultural counties of Ireland.

It did not take long for English and Scottish football clubs to become professional by the end of the nineteenth century, although it would be many years before professional footballers reaped the benefits of their talent in terms of earnings and freedom of contract. This followed a campaign fronted by Jimmy Hill, at the time a Fulham player and chair of the Professional Footballers Association who went on to become manager of Coventry City and the 'face of football' of BBC Television. The maximum wage, at that time £20 a week, was abolished. As increasingly more money has poured into the British game and into the pockets of footballers and their agents, a larger proportion of players in the Premier League are now from overseas.

Three of the twelve clubs in the NIFL – Glentoran, Linfield and Larne – have recently become full-time professional, although the small attendances at matches restricts, directly and indirectly, the scope for expansion to further clubs.

In contrast, Gaelic football has shown no similar expansion, and has remained local, national, and amateur even at its highest level. Its status should also be contextualised in the history of the emergence of an independent Ireland, where promotion of the Irish language and culture was encouraged. It retains its nationalist ethos. Its website (consulted in February 2023) states that its purpose is to 'promote Gaelic games, culture and lifelong participation as a community-based, volunteer-led organisation which enriches lives and communities'. It qualifies this by being 'open to diverse opinions while respecting our Irish heritage and language'. It also aims to 'promote Irish music, song and dance, and the Irish language as an integral part of its objectives'.

Casement Park, the Belfast GAA stadium has been closed and deteriorating since 2013. Attempts are being made to develop it into a first-class, modern, 35,000 capacity stadium although, as I write, its planning application has been delayed by local protests. One of its stated intentions is to broaden its user base and there are tentative plans to include it in a joint British/ Irish bid to host the 2028 Euro soccer championships.[49] It has also been suggested that it might make a back-up to Ravenhill for Ulster Rugby rather than the current alternative, the RDS ground in Dublin.[50] While these proposals offer a step to inclusiveness and are to be welcomed, one worries about the prospect of thousands of Protestant soccer and rugby supporters making their way up the Falls Road. Soccer fans might be particularly worrying, given the sectarianism that still accompanies the sport.

Eddie's question might be reframed in a counterfactual way. What if I had been brought up a

Catholic and the question was why I never played association football? This seems a more unlikely question since many Catholics do play football for enjoyment and do represent teams in Northern Ireland at amateur, professional and international levels.

Nevertheless, the alternative question might lead me to recall that playing 'foreign' games was proscribed for many years by the GAA and this would explain why I never played soccer. Thus, there is a clear asymmetry between the two questions. This is also apparent when reading the Ulster GAA Chief Executive, Brian McAvoy's statement to the *Belfast Telegraph* that he would like to see more Protestants joining the organisation, which raises the question whether Protestants would be happy to play in grounds and clubs named after republicans and IRA members. Gaelic games come with nationalist baggage.[51]

Why I never thought of playing Gaelic football is straightforward to answer on a personal level but it raises many questions about the country and city in which I was born and brought up. I hope that I have managed to identify some of the factors that contributed to this.

The enjoyment of football has played an important part in my life from early boyhood to the present day. I was fortunate at Keele to be able to watch top-division English league football at Stoke City's Victoria Ground, for very reasonable prices in those days, and to live in Belfast and Cardiff where it was straightforward to attend international matches, involving all the home nations and Brazil, Germany, Mexico, Belgium, and Hungary.

My playing days were long past by then, five-a-side at Penwortham Leisure Centre being my swansong. However, I have obtained pleasure from watching future generations take up the sport. John played for Penwortham Boys and Middleforth Primary School when we were at Preston. After we came to South Wales he played as a centre-back for Dinas Powys in the Barry and District League and the Cardiff and District League. He was selected to represent both leagues in representative matches against other counties. His team won all three trophies that were available to them in the Vale of Glamorgan Under-15 age group and won the Cardiff and District Under-16 age group League. After this, John and other boys from Dinas Powys played for Inter Cable Tel in the South Wales Youth League before he went to Oxford and played for Somerville College. More recently. I have been to watch my grandson Otis, one of the two sons of Eddie and Beth, play at the famous Hackney Marshes in London.

Eddie's question threw me because *not* watching the Gaelic form of football is something that I had never thought about, despite it being the sport of choice of a large number of my fellow citizens in Northern Ireland, with major matches played in my city, and while I attended university alongside many members of the minority community.

I had no choice in the matter of being born into one community in a divided society, and it was some time before I thought of my world in terms of this division. The American psychologist George A. Kelly would characterise this in terms of my lack of a *personal construct* for Protestant versus Catholic. By this he means that I did not use this construct to divide up my world in order to understand it. It is a widely available construct in Northern Ireland although we must take into account that constructs are *personal* and fit into an individual's system of constructs in diverse ways. For example, it might be more salient for one person than for another, or at one time rather than another. Its range of application can vary; we might be friendly with *individuals* from the other community but hold negative attitudes about the community itself. Kelly devised a method – the Repertory Grid Technique – to explore individuals' sets of constructs.

The construct is less salient in contemporary English society, nevertheless it was one of the major issues in British history after King Henry VIII's break from Rome, the sacking of monasteries and the persecution of Catholics and it persists in such matters as the ineligibility of a Roman Catholic to become monarch. Constructs are fluid. I acquired and elaborated upon the protestant-catholic construct as I was growing up while someone like Derek Dougan learnt to construe the division differently after he relocated to England.

Once again, it is misleading to focus on religion as the driver of sectarianism. It is only one aspect of a broader difference between the two communities, one that has the history that I have explored in this essay.

There are increasing attempts to bring both sports closer together. In his memoir, Willie Anderson describes Dungannon rugby club reaching out to local GAA players in the hope of widening the club's player and support base, and he points to the pleasure that rugby supporters took in County Tyrone's success at Gaelic football. He was happy for his son to play rugby at school and GAA in their home village. He also describes a charity match between the GAA and rugby teams in Dungannon, half of the match played as rugby and the other half as Gaelic football.

The Northern Ireland Department of Communities has entered into partnership with Sport Northern Ireland that includes a Sport Matters Implementation Group that aims to bring together sports within its jurisdiction including representatives from the IFA and the GAA. A newspaper report of October 2008 shows Roy Millar of the IFA and Danny Murphy of the Ulster Council GAA at an IFA Schools Coaches Training Day in Magherafelt that involved both codes.[52] A redeveloped Casement Park might potentially facilitate this process.

An explicitly non-sectarian soccer club, Antrim Rovers, was formed by food-safety scientist Professor Christopher Elliott of Queen's University Belfast when he was horrified to witness sectarianism after his son began playing football. The club now runs twelve teams, for men and boys, women and girls, and has 250 registered players.

Yet there remain many hurdles, particularly the continuing uncertainties about political stability in Northern Ireland and their impact on the segregation of communities and schooling. Sinn Féin won sufficient seats in the last Assembly election to nominate the First Minister and form a government, but its opening statements have been to reaffirm its commitment to a united Ireland, hardly a recipe for defusing tension. The DUP has become obsessed with the Protocol and its aftermath, and is unlikely to cooperate with the government until matters are resolved to its satisfaction.

The political outlook does not look promising. Tension between the two communities has not disappeared and is frequently exploited by political parties and organisations for their own ends. The association between the GAA and Irish nationalism, republicanism and Catholicism remains a deterrent for loyalists. The identification of the IFA and the major clubs in the Irish League with the flying of British and Ulster flags and banners at international matches is a deterrent for many Catholics. Many who travel across the sea to watch Celtic or Manchester United would be reluctant to attend an NIFL match.

It is surely remarkable that local football of both codes managed to continue to play throughout the years of the Troubles and that violence connected to football has not been more common. Crowd misbehaviour including racist chanting and violence is not restricted to Northern Ireland, and its travelling fans behave much better abroad than do, for example, English supporters. There too, the aggression is accompanied by English nationalism, the display of flags and other emblems, and the chanting of offensive slogans.

It is remarkable too the degree to which much of civil life has recovered in Northern Ireland. This is after thirty years of deaths, of atrocities and the disruption of daily routines when everyone was searched before entering the city centre and going into shops, and one could never predict when and where a bomb might be detonated. Nowadays, citizens see killers released from prison or occupying prominent political positions. There is currently a vigorous social and cultural scene and this is perhaps where hope for the future is to be found, rather in the current political realm, where few seem prepared to move on from entrenched positions and where the threat of violence is hinted at whenever parties fail to get their own way. The 'not an inch' mentality is still present, to the frustration of many, including those in the business sector.

This can be illustrated by the current stand-off over the post-Brexit arrangements. As it stands in April 2023, the UK government and the EU have reached an agreement – the Windsor Framework – so the situation may have changed by the time you read this. The solution on the table offers a unique opportunity for the Northern Ireland economy to reap the benefits of access to both the EU and UK markets. Yet it is a badge of honour for many loyalists that nothing should be allowed to weaken the link with Great Britain even though, or perhaps because, the threat to the union is symbolic rather than real. Where the Westminster government seeks to negotiate a practical settlement with the EU, that is, to reach some form of compromise, there is no evidence that the DUP will accept any solution, however favourable it might be economically, that represents any distinction between Northern Ireland and Great Britain, between Finaghy and Finchley. As Sir Jeffrey Donaldson, leader of the DUP is quoted as saying, following the rejection by the UK Supreme Court of the case brought by loyalists that the Protocol is illegal, that the Protocol 'represents an existential threat to the future of Northern Ireland's place within the union'.[53] There are many within the UK Conservative Party who would support this stance.

The border remains in place constitutionally, Protocol, Framework or not, but to my mind it would surely become less significant psychologically and socially as its economic and cultural import dwindles.

Citizens of Northern Ireland can choose to be British, Irish or both. Given these circumstances, a united Ireland might become less relevant.

There is always the possibility that events can produce surprising changes. There are many imponderables, even if one restricts attention to Britain and Ireland rather than international issues such as the climate crisis and the impact of Russia's invasion of Ukraine. From the North's perspective, several changes are possible. The Brexit negotiations, particularly over the Protocol and now the Windsor Framework, might bring about a solution that is acceptable to all parties. Perhaps the UK will negotiate a closer economic relationship with the EU. Changes to governance in Stormont might bolster the emerging tendency for centrist parties to win more seats. The demographic change in the populations of self-identified Catholics and Protestants, may, if the current trend continues, also have unforeseen consequences. The superiority of health and welfare arrangements in the North – one of the principal attractions of the Union that crosses denominational lines – might disappear in the light of the Conservative Party's determination to bring in privatisation and finance the health service through private insurance schemes, probably using the NHS title as brand name rather than a depiction of reality.

There is a tendency among younger voters to reject the extremist positions in Stormont taken by the DUP and Sinn Féin, but we don't know whether this will be maintained as they grow older. The police and courts might get to grip with paramilitary crime. This remains challenging because these gangs are embedded in their communities, citizens including victims are reluctant to give evidence because of realistic fear of reprisals, and the gangs are welcomed by many as defenders of their community.

From the perspective of the South, the dramatic recent development has been in the relationship of the state and society to the Roman Catholic Church, brought about in part by changing moral values within the population and in part by the series of scandals involving the Church, in sexual abuse and in the maltreatment of women and children in its care. Membership of the EU and the increase in immigration from overseas may also contribute to these changes and produce a more diverse society. Time will tell. The Irish economy is currently in good health and it benefits from membership of the EU. However, there is no guarantee that the strength of the economy will continue, given its current reliance on foreign investment from high-tech companies.

Common to jurisdictions North and South is the rise of Sinn Féin in elections since the Good Friday Agreement. If and when Stormont resumes without another election, Sinn Féin will hold the office of First Minister and will be able to appoint other ministers in the Executive. South of the border, the party's progress forced Fine Gael and Fianna Fáil to share government for the first time – the antagonism between the two parties dates to the Irish Civil War. Sinn Féin won 37 seats with 24.5% of the popular vote; Fianna Fáil 38 seats (22.2%) and Fine Gael 35 seats (21%).

It is difficult to predict the future were Sinn Féin to be in office in both jurisdictions at the same time, other than to suggest that the issue of a united Ireland would be high on its agenda, with all the anxieties that would cause in the North (and among substantial numbers in the South). It is also difficult to know whether the rise in its support has the same meanings or causes on both sides of the border, and to what extent its rise reflects moves away from the centre towards extremes in elections across Europe, a trend that is also evident within the Republican Party in the US and the Conservative Party in the UK.

All in all, my experience of playing football has been one of pleasure in participation rather than having any marked success. I have been somewhat of a geek in my delight in meeting sports heroes (in addition to those mentioned already, I have met Harry Gregg and Hubert Barr, another Northern Ireland international (with whom I played an impromptu kick-about in the garden of our rented holiday bungalow in Ballyreagh, outside Portrush – see the photograph of the garden on page 142). I chatted in Botanic Avenue in Belfast with Norman Uprichard, Distillery, Swindon, Portsmouth and NI international goalkeeper, and, in Blackpool, with Stanley Mortensen, an England international centre-forward who scored a hat-trick for Blackpool in the 1953 FA Cup Final in 1953, the first player to do so at a Wembley final, even though his contribution tends to be overlooked as the match is now described as the 'Matthews final' highlighting Sir Stanley Matthews winning the medal after so many years of trying.

I have lived much longer outside Northern Ireland than inside it and only close family ties and life-long friendships made the period of the Troubles a reality for me. Yet my experience of life and football has been coloured by the society in which I was born and lived in until my mid-twenties. For much of my childhood I was unaware that this experience was exceptional. I was brought up in a Protestant district, attended

Protestant schools and played for a Protestant-church-linked team within a society where the distinction between Protestant and Roman Catholic had profound significance.

The Ulster Unionist Party and the Orange Order were significant organisations in our community and the 12th July was and remains the principal, annual celebration of Protestant hegemony. Along with my family I watched several of its annual marches along the Lisburn Road on their way to the 'field' at Finaghy, sometimes having pointed out to me 'celebrities' such as Unionist MPs and leaders of the Order. We would retire to my grandfather's house after the march had passed.

Catholics were 'other' as I was growing up even if we expressed no hostility towards individuals, yet beyond our family there was no shortage of nasty names to call them or prejudiced remarks about them. I was in contact with only one boy who was a Catholic until I went up to university, where I did make good friends across the divide. Any hopes that Terence O'Neill would bring about meaningful changes were soon dashed. Indeed, any unionist leader who has made any attempt at negotiation has been quickly ejected from his position by his party – O'Neill, Chichester-Clark, Faulkner, Trimble. DUP leaders are currently struggling with the consequences of Brexit, and have made rapid changes in leadership after Reverend Paisley's departure.

Progress to reduce segregation in education has been slow. The Conference hosted by Queen's University in April 2023 to celebrate the 25th anniversary of the Good Friday Agreement was successful, attracting significant speakers including Bill and Hillary Clinton and Senator George Mitchell. The consensus was that considerable progress has been made in reducing violence and in reducing barriers between the communities although the failure of the Assembly to provide continuity in governance was regretted (the Assembly was suspended because of the DUP's withdrawal of support for procedure). Yet, Hillary Clinton's conferral of honorary degrees on those responsible for the establishment of the Limavady Shared Education Campus, bringing together on a single campus two schools from across the divide, Limavady High School and St Mary's Limavady, provided an optimistic note on which to end the conference. Rather than 'not an inch', 'inching forward' might be the motto.

Living in England and Wales, I attend Catholic weddings and funerals, often unaware until I arrive that they are Catholic ceremonies; It never occurs to me to enquire beforehand. Ireland has a different history from the rest of the United Kingdom in this respect and I hope I have managed to convey something of the nature of this difference and why it has led to two communities within the same city, including me, playing, watching, following and ignoring different codes of football.

APPENDIX 1

Numbers of seats won by the three principal parties in the general elections, 1885-1910

	Liberal	Conservative	IPP [a]
1885	319	247	86
1886	192	393[b]	86
1892	271	314	84[c]
1895	177	411	82[d]
1900	183	402	76
1906	397	156[e]	82
1910, January	274	272	71
1910, December	272	271	74

a Irish Parliamentary Party

b Liberals who supported the Union formed an alliance with the Conservative Party. The election results showed a large increase in the number of Conservative and Unionist seats and a decline in the number of Liberal seats, relative to the 1885 election.

c The IPP split following the scandal surrounding its leader Charles Stewart Parnell's affair with Kitty O'Shea. In 1892, 72 of the members returned were for the anti-Parnell Irish National Federation (INF) and 9 were for the pro-Parnell Irish National League (INL).

d In the 1895 election, the INF won 70 seats and the INL won 12 seats.

e The Conservatives were divided over the issue of free trade.

Founded in 1891, the Irish Unionist Alliance, representing unionists, won between 17 and 19 of the 103 Irish seats in these elections.

*

The crucial post-war general election in 1918 produced a distinctive and unusual set of results. The results were: Conservative 379 sets; Liberal coalition 127; other Liberals 36; Labour 57, Sinn Féin 73; IPP 7.

Lloyd George, who led the Liberal-Conservative coalition that had governed during the war, gave his party members the opportunity to 'take the coupon', i.e.,', to stand for the coalition in the forthcoming election. This effectively split the Liberal Party. The Labour Party was beginning to make an impression.

Sinn Féin also ran and took nearly all the seats previously won by the IPP, INF and INL. This anticipates the Party's success in recent elections north and south of the border. The Party continues to refuse to take the seats it has won in Westminster.

Being an active member of a church was an important part of my parents' life as well as of the lives of my mother's sister, Maud and her husband Norman, and of her brother, Jack, his wife Honor and their families. Uncle Jack was a Methodist minister so he and Honor had many duties and responsibilities within the Church.

Not all self-identified Protestants attend church and the numbers have been in decline over the years. When pressed about this, Reverend Paisley asserted that he was defending the Protestant way of life. It is difficult to know how this can be defined other than in terms of defending Protestants from Catholicism. Is it better to have no religion than to be of the wrong sort of religion?

How did my mother come to have an address at 80 North Parade? My research suggests that the connection was through Ormeau Road Methodist Church. I learned that David Tees was a leader of this congregation. He is also described as prominent in Methodist circles in the city. He was married with three grown-up children, two boys and a girl, and lived at 80 North Parade. His wife died in 1939, a year before my parents' wedding. Might my mother have acted as housekeeper for Mr Tees following his bereavement? Both his sons served in the war. The elder boy, also called David, was killed in action in November 1942 and a huge funeral service was held in Ormeau Road church. My brother David was born in January 1943. Might this have influenced my parents' choice of name for their first child? Tees died suddenly in Antwerp in 1953, returning from a visit to the US. He was not a resident of North Parade at the time.

Measuring residential segregation

The Dissimilarity Index (D) is one measure of the degree of segregation among groups within a given population, for example districts in a city. Conceptually, it assigns a point on a numerical scale to measure the amount of change that would need to take place within a district so that it would be representative of the proportion in the city as a whole.

For example, say that the city of Belfast is made up of 50% Catholics and 50% Protestants. If a particular district also had 50-50, then the Index would be zero for that district and no change is needed. If the proportion in a district is 100% Protestant, then D would be at its maximum, 100.

In the study by Doherty and Poole, described here, Holywood, a seaside town to the east of Belfast had D =16.0. Predominantly Catholic Belfast West had D = 63.9, the highest value of D in the study.

Interpretation ought to take into account the size of the units since small units might yield higher indices.

For comparison, local authority data for England in 2021, comparing the White and Non-White populations, give a mean D value of 45.7. The value for the South East region is 35.8 and for Yorkshire and Humberside is 54.3, the highest mean. (Data from the Department of Levelling Up, Housing and Communities.)

(https://lginform.local.gov.uk/reports/lgastandard?mod-area=E92000001&mod-group=AllRegions_England&mod-metric=9040&mod-type=namedComparisonGroup)

NOTES

I appreciate that notes can be irritating to some readers but deemed essential by others who wish to identify the sources for points raised. They can also be useful for further reading. Feel free to skip them.

1 Tóibín, pp. 107, 126
2 Foster, *Modern History*, p. 465
3 Gavin Willacy, *Guardian* online, March 16, 2018
4 Paul Keane, *The Irish Times* online, January 27, 2023
5 Foster, *Modern Ireland*, p. 449
6 Henry McDonald, *The Observer* online, November 18, 2001
7 Tóibín, pp. 80-81
8 Niall McCoy, *Cross' and Choppers: 50 years on from the British occupation of Crossmaglen's grounds*, RTÉ, Sunday November 14, 2021. www.ret.ie
9 James Quinn, *Dictionary of Irish Biography*, 2014
10 Bairner & Walker
11 *Prospect* magazine, December 8, 2008
12 *Morning Star* online, accessed January 13, 2023
13 Alex Mills, *Sunday Life*, January 9, 2017
14 *Belfast Telegraph* online, January 16, 2020
15 *The Newsletter*, Retro rewind, April 23, 2020
16 Steven Beacon, *Belfast Telegraph* online, December 4, 2022
17 Keith Bailie, *Belfast Telegraph* online, February 23, 2023
18 quoted by Gerry Moriarty, *The Irish Times*, April 9, 2016
19 Richard Smith, *Mirror* online, September 8, 2011
20 Dougan, p. 20
21 Bowler, p. 27. There is a blue plaque at 49 Grace Avenue
22 Blanchflower, pp. 14, 19
23 Conroy, pp. 35-47

24 Dougan, p. 60

25 Bowker, p. 134

26 O'Driscoll, pp. 43-44

27 McKittrick & McVea, p.27

28 Thomas Henry, *A History of* the *Belfast Riots*, 1864, quoted by Craig, 1999, p. 309

29 Sean O'Faolain, *An Irish Journey*, 1940, quoted by Craig, p. 320

30 Clarkson, p. 176

31 Moloney & Pollak, p. 296

32 Clarkson, p. 132

33 Allison Morris, *Irish News*, February 20, 2016

34 McCrudden et al., p. 136

35 Diarmaid Ferriter, *Irish Times*, November 28, 2015, p. 14

36 Shovlin, p. 177

37 Foster, *Luck of the Irish*

38 Cairns, p. 123

39 Smyth et al.

40 https://factcheckni.org/articles/do-far-more-young-people-in-northern-ireland-have-no-qualifications-compared-with-peers-in-england

41 Borooah & Knox

42 Mania, pp. 87-102

43 Tausch et al.

44 Hughes & Loader, 2021

45 Gallagher, 2018

46 Johnston, *Queen's Policy Engagement*, 2021

47 Shovlin, p. 454; McGahern watched the FA Cup Final in William Blake's Bar, Enniskillen

48 *Belfast Live* online, January 20, 2023, www.belfastlive.co.uk

49 John Breslin, *The Irish News* online, November 17, 2022

50 Jonathan Bradley, *Belfast Telegraph* online, December 21, 2022

51 *Belfast Telegraph* online, April 14, 2023

52 Oliver McVeigh, *Sportsfile*, sportsfile.com/RP0063102

53 Lisa O'Carroll, *Guardian* online, February 8, 2023

BIBLIOGRAPHY

Anderson, Willie with Brendan Fanning. *Crossing the Line*. Liverpool: Reach Sport, 2022.

Bairner, A. and G. Walker. Football and society in Northern Ireland: Linfield Football Club and the case of Gerry Morgan. *Soccer & Society*, 2010, 2 (1) 81-88.

Belfast Agreement. *The Belfast Agreement: An Agreement Reached at the Multi-Party Talks on Northern Ireland*. London: The Stationery Office.

Best, George. *Blessed. The Autobiography*. London: Ebury Press, 2001.

Blanchflower, Danny. *Danny Blanchflower's Soccer Book*. London: Frederick Muller Limited, 1959.

Borooah, Vani H. and Colin Knox. Inequality, segregation and poor performance: the education system in Northern Ireland. *Educational Review*, 2017, 69, no. 3, 318-336.

Bowler, Dave. *Danny Blanchflower. A Biography of a Visionary*. London: Vista, 1997.

Brodie, Malcolm, *100 Years of Irish Football*. Belfast: Blackstaff Press, 1980.

Brodie, Malcolm (editor). *Northern Ireland Soccer Yearbook. 2009*. Belfast: Ulster Tatler Publications, 2011-2012.

Brown, Daniel. Linfield's 'Hawk of Peace': pre-ceasefires reconciliation in Irish League football. *Soccer & Society*, 2017, 18, nos. 5-6, 679-692.

Brownlow, G. Industrial policy in Northern Ireland: past, present and future. *Economic and Social Review*, 2020, 52, no. 3, 407-424.

Burns, Stephanie, Ruth Leitch, and Joanne Hughes. *Education Inequalities in Northern Ireland. Summary Report*, 2015. https://www.equalityni.org/ECNI/media/ECNI/Public ations/Delivering%20Equality/EducationInequality-SummaryReport.pdf

Cairns, Ed, *Caught in Crossfire. Children and the Northern Ireland Conflict*. Belfast: Appletree Press, 1987.

Cameron, Lord (Chairman). *Disturbances in Northern Ireland, Report of the Commission Appointed by the Governor of Northern Ireland*. Belfast: HMSO, 1969.

Chinoy Mike, *Are You With Me? Kevin Boyle and the Rise of the Human Rights Movement*. Dublin: The Lilliput Press, 2020.

Clarkson L. A. *A University in Troubled Times, Queen's Belfast, 1945-2000*. Dublin: Four Courts Press, 2004.

Collins, Tony. Welsh codebreakers in the inter-war years, 2018. https://tony-collins.squarespace.com

Conroy, Terry. *You don't remember me, do you? The Autobiography of Terry Conroy*. Durrington: Pitch Publishing, 2015.

Craig, Patricia (editor). *The Belfast Anthology*. Belfast: Blackstaff Press, 1999.

Cronin, Mike. Catholics and Sport in Northern Ireland. Exclusiveness or Inclusiveness. In Tara Magdalinski and Timothy J. L. Chandler (editors). *With God on their Side* (pp. 20-34). London: Routledge, 2002.

Crozier, F. P. *A Brass Hat in No Man's Land*. London: Jonathan Cape, 1930.

Doherty, Peter and Michael A. Poole. Ethnic residential segregation in Belfast, Northern Ireland, 1971-1991. *The Geographical Review*, 8, no.4, 520-536, 1997.

Dougan, Derek. *The Sash He Never Wore*. St Albans: Granada Books, 1972.

Fanning, Ronan *Éamon De Valera. A Will to Power*. London: Faber and Faber, 2015.

Ferriter, Diarmaid. *The Border. The Legacy of a Century of Irish Politics*. London: Profile Books, 2019.

Foster. R. F. *Modern Ireland 1600-1972*, London: Penguin, 1989.

Foster, R. F. *Luck and the Irish. A brief history of change, 1970-2000*. London: Penguin, 2008.

Gallagher, Tony. Building a shared future from a divided past: Promoting peace through education in Northern Ireland. In Gavriel Salomon and Ed Cairns (editors) *Handbook on Peace Education* (pp. 241-252). New York: Psychology Press, 2010.

Gallagher, Tony. Shared education produces positive community impacts, *VIEW*, 45, 2018.

Harris, Rosemary. *Prejudice and Tolerance in Ulster: A Study of Neighbours and "Strangers" in a Border Community.* Manchester: Manchester University Press, 1972.

Hawkins, Richard. Frank Percy Crozier. *Dictionary of Irish Biography*, 2009. https://doi.org/10.3318/dib.002261.v1

Hiles, J. Clarence. *A History of Senior Cricket in Ulster*. Comber, Co. Down. Hilltop Publications, 2004.

Hiles, J. Clarence. Gone but not forgotten – Margaret Waring. *The Ulster Cricketer*, July 22, 2020.

Hughes, Joanne and Rebecca Loader. Is academic selection in Northern Ireland a barrier to social cohesion? *Research Papers in Education*, 2022. https://doi.org/10.1080/026

Hughes, Joanne and Rebecca Loader. Shared education: a case study in social cohesion. *Research Papers in Education*, 2021. https://doi.org/10.1080/02671522.2021.1961303

Johnston, Jennifer. Integrated Education Policy: Where is the political will. *Queen's Policy Engagement*, September 8, 2021. http://qpol.qub.ac.uk/integrated-education-ppolict-where-is-the-political-will

Joyce, James. *Dubliners*. London: Penguin, 1996. First published 1914.

Kelly, George A. A brief introduction to personal construct theory. *Costruttivismi*, 4, 3025, 2017. httpp://doi.org:10.23826/2017.01.003.025

Mallon, Seamus. *A Shared Home Place*. Dublin: The Lilliput Press, 2019.

Mania, Eric W., Samuel L. Gaertner, Blake M. Riek, John F. Dovidio, Marika. J. Lamoreaux, and Stacy A. Direso. Intergroup contact. Implications for peace education. In Gavriel Salomon and Ed Cairns (editors), *Handbook on Peace Education* (pp. 87-102). New York: Psychology Press. 2010.

McClelland, Gillian. *Pioneering women. Riddel Hall and Queen's University Belfast*. Belfast: Ulster Historical Foundation, 2005.

McCrudden, Christopher, Robert Ford and Anthony Heath. The impact of affirmative action agreements. In Osborne, Bob and Ian Shuttleworth (eds.) *Fair Employment in Northern Ireland; A Generation On* (pp. 122-150). Belfast: Blackstaff Press, 2004.

McKay, Susan. Diary: Pro-Union Unionists. *London Review of Books*, 2021, 43, no. 5, 44-45.

McKittrick, David and David McVea. *Making Sense of the Troubles*. London, Penguin, 2012.

Megven, Paul G. *The 1964 West Belfast 'Tricolour Riots*. https://thebrokenelbow.com/2020/08/20/the-divis-street-riots-of-1964/

Messenger, Charles. *Broken Sword. The Tumultuous Life of General Frank Crozier, 1879-1937*. Barnsley: Pen & Sword Books Ltd, 2013.

Miéville, China. *The City & The City*. London: Macmillan, 2009.

Moloney, Ed and Andy Pollak. *Paisley*. Swords, Co. Dublin: Poolbeg, 1986.

Mulholland, Marc. *Terence O'Neill*. Dublin: University College Dublin Press, 2013.

Murphy, Dervla. *A Place Apart: Northern Ireland in the 1970s*. London: John Murray, 1978.

Northern Ireland Office and Foreign, Commonwealth and Development Office. Wilton Park Summit, WP 1994. *A new confident and inclusive Northern Ireland, 2022*. https://www.wiltonpark.org.uk/wp-content/uploads/2022/08/WP11994-Report.pdf

O'Callaghan, Eimar. *Belfast Days. A Teenage Diary 1972*. Salling, Co. Kildare: Merrion Press, 2014.

O'Driscoll, Dennis. *Stepping Stones. Interviews with Seamus Heaney*. London: Faber and Faber, 2009.

O'Leary, Brendan. *Making Sense of a United Ireland, Should it Happen? How Might it Happen?* London: Sandycove, 2022.

Osborne, Bob and Ian Shuttleworth (eds.) *Fair Employment in Northern Ireland; A Generation On*. Belfast: Blackstaff Press, 2004.

Patterson, Glenn. Once *Upon a Hill. Love in Troubled Times*. London: Bloomsbury, 2008.

Patterson, Henry. *Ireland Since 1939. Persistence of Conflict*. London: Penguin, 2006.

Police Service of Northern Ireland. *Equality Scheme [Equality, Diversity and Good Relations Strategy, 2017-2022]*, 2022. https://www.psni.police.uk/sites/default/files/2022-09/section-75-equality-scheme-booklet.pdf

Pollak, Andy. Getting There, *Dublin Review of Books*, 149, no. 2, December 2022.

Paulin, Tom. *The Wind Dog*. London: Faber and Faber, 1999.

Quinn, James. Johnny Carey. *Dictionary of Irish Biography*, 2014.

Roberts, Benjamin. *Northern Ireland's journey to their first world cup*, November 7, 2017. https://worldfootballindex.com/2017/11/northern-irelands-journey-first-world-cup/

Roulston, Stephen. *Transforming Education. Education across the island of Ireland. Comparing systems and outcomes*. Ulster University Briefing Paper 14, 2021.

Russell, Raymond. Employment profiles of Protestants and Catholics: A decade of monitoring. In Osborne, Bob and Ian Shuttleworth (eds.) *Fair Employment in Northern Ireland; A Generation On* (pp. 24-48). Belfast: Blackstaff Press, 2004.

Schubotz, Dirk and Gillian Robinson. Cross-community integration and mixing: does it make a difference? *ARK Research Update*, 43, April 2006.

Shovlin, Frank (editor). *The Letters of John McGahern*. London, Faber: 2021.

Smyth, Emer, Anne Devlin, Adele Bergin, and Seamus McGuinness. *A North-South Comparison of Education Systems: Lessons for Policy*. Dublin: The Economic and Social Research Institute (ESRI), Research Series, no. 138, 2022.

Tajfel, Henri and John C. Turner. An integrative theory of inter-group conflict. In W. G. Austin and S. Worchel (editors) *The Psychology of Intergroup Relations* (pp. 33-47). Monterey, California: Brooks/Cole, 1979.

Tausch, Nicole, Tania Tam, Miles Hewstone, Jared Kenworthy, and Ed Cairns. Individual-level and group-level mediators of contact effects in Northern Ireland: The moderating role of social identification. *British Journal of Social Psychology*, 2007, 46, 541-556.

Tóibín, Colm. *Bad Blood*. London: Picador, 2001.

Zajonc, Robert. Attitudinal effects of mere exposure. *Journal of Personality and Social Psychology*, 1968, 9, no. 2, 1-27.

I would not have been able to complete this essay without Sandra's support, particularly during my spell of illness that encouraged me to write it. Particular thanks to Eddie, for starting me thinking about sectarianism in football and for inspiring me to research into it. I also thank the late Professor Ed Cairns, whose research I have quoted. We were contemporaries in the psychology department at Queen's and we shared many conversations about Northern Ireland over the years, at conferences in Denver, Colorado, and Tampa, Florida. Sadly, Ed died in 2012. I have benefited from the meticulous record-keeping in the Year Books on Northern Ireland soccer produced by the late Dr Malcolm Brodie, MBE.

The cover photograph of the author at the football pitches in Ormeau Park was taken in the early 1970s by Sandra Crozier. The top photograph on the back cover is of Murphy's Engineering Company football team in the 1950s, photographer unknown. My father is on the left of the back row; the author as a boy is on the back row right. The lower back cover photograph is of the KRA football side in 1971, photographer unknown. The author is standing in the back row, at the right.

The photograph on page 90 of the back entry at 24 North Parade is reproduced courtesy of Google and to the best of my knowledge meets its criteria for inclusion in a book. The photograph on page 142 of the three brothers, Raymond, David and Alan, with our mother in the background holding a neighbour's baby, is from our family collection, as is the photograph below it of the author on vacation in the bungalow at Ballyreagh.

I am conscious of covering a great deal of material in this essay, much more than I had set out to do, and I have introduced a range of topics that have been meticulously researched by others. I hope that I have done justice to their work and apologise if I have misinterpreted any of it.